The Abortion Prevention Manual

The Ultimate Battleplan for the Body of Christ to Win the War Against Abortion

Brandi & Robyn Cunningham

The Abortion Prevention Manual: The Ultimate Battleplan for the Body of Christ to Win the War Against Abortion

Copyright 2024 by Robyn and Brandi Cunningham

Published by Robyn and Brandi Cunningham

All rights reserved. No part of this book may be reproduced, stored in a retrieval system, or transmitted in any form or by any means—electronic, mechanical, photocopy, recording, or otherwise—without prior written permission of the copyright owner. To obtain permission for use, please contact us at firesidegrace@yahoo.com

Unless otherwise noted, all Scripture quotations taken from The Holy Bible, New International Version® NIV® Copyright © 1973, 1978, 1984, 2011 by Biblica, Inc. Used with permission. All rights reserved worldwide.

Scripture quotations marked (NKJV) are taken from the NEW KING JAMES VERSION (NKJV): Scripture taken from the NEW KING JAMES VERSION®. Copyright© 1982 by Thomas Nelson, Inc. Used by permission. All rights reserved.

Scripture quotations marked (KJV) are from the King James Version and are in the public domain.

Scripture quotations marked (ESV) taken from The Holy Bible, English Standard Version. ESV® Text Edition: 2016. Copyright © 2001 by Crossway Bibles, a publishing ministry of Good News Publishers.

Scripture quotations marked (AMP) are taken from the Amplified Bible Copyright © 2015 by The Lockman Foundation, La Habra, CA 90631. All rights reserved.

Scripture quotations marked (MSG) taken from The Message, Copyright © 1993, 2002, 2018 by Eugene H. Peterson.

All emphases in Scripture are the author's own.

ISBNs: 978-1-953143-09-9 (Paperback)

       978-1-953143-10-5 (eBook)

Printed in the U.S.A.

We dedicate this book to a few different people:

To the 60 million plus babies that have lost their lives in the worst holocaust since 1945;

To Lindy Jones, who taught Brandi more than any book could, and never ceases to love people extraordinarily. You're brave and you have impacted more people than you will ever know. Thank you, for being her mentor.

And lastly, to Jarrod Breshears. Jarrod bravely replaced Brandi's monthly income for a few months so that we could solely work on this book and prevent as many abortions as possible. Jarrod lost his life tragically in the battle to covid-19 and we are honoring him and what he believed by continuing the fight against the loss of so many perfectly innocent lives.

We could never thank each of you enough.

We're here until the end to fight the good fight and we hope it honors you each by doing so.

Love,

Brandi and Robyn

Contents

Introduction	God's Heart Regarding Abortion	7
Chapter 1	The Current State of Abortion, Nationally and Globally	11
Chapter 2	Abortion Abolition and Abortion Prevention	17
Chapter 3	Abortion Prevention Crash Course: The Lies Families Believe and How to Counteract Them	25
Chapter 4	The Role of Single Parenting with Regard to Abortion Rates	33
Chapter 5	Current Abortion Types (Medical and *Natural*) and All About the Reversal Pill	37
Chapter 6	Long-Term Effects of an Abortion of Any Type	41
Chapter 7	What the Bible Teaches About an Unborn Child	45
Chapter 8	Scripture Arguments People Use to Defend Abortion Rights	49
Chapter 9	Waves of Feminism and Rape Culture: Why They are Important	53
Chapter 10	Understanding the Biblical Argument for Purity	61
Chapter 11	Birth Control: A Cultural Controversy	67
Chapter 12	The Biblical View of Adoption	71
Chapter 13	How To Minister to Someone Who Has Had an Abortion	79
Chapter 14	The Role of the Church in Politics from a Biblical Standpoint	83

Introduction

God's Heart Regarding Abortion

One night, before I (Robyn) went to bed, I asked God to show me His heart about abortion. I had a dream that I was in a huge church, and I was part of the worship team. An old friend of mine from school was going to have a baby, and he was part of the worship team as well. The worship leader would not let him lead worship because he was in sin; he was not married but was expecting a child. They rejected him and would not even recognize him. I saw in his heart that this troubled him. I tried to talk to the worship leader about it, and they implied that I should not reach out to him because he was in sin. He decided he was going to keep the baby, do the right thing, work, and raise the child. He was determined to abandon his old lifestyle and become a responsible adult, no matter the cost—even though his friends were trying to convince him that keeping the baby was a mistake. Michael looked worn out and tired, but he wanted to do what was right.

I talked to him and said, "Congratulations, man! Having kids changed my life so much, and it has been a great blessing. It is not easy at first, but it is totally worth it."

His friends ganged up on him and began telling him what a mistake it was to have a baby now. He was in school, he was part of a worship team, he had not lived life yet, he was not ready to settle down, he could not party anymore, he did not make enough money, he had no house, and he was not married. Tired and worn out from their harassment, he went outside to his trailer in the parking lot to rest. While he was asleep, they hitched his trailer to a guy named Thomas's truck and began to recklessly drive away without regard for anyone else. Michael left the church that abandoned him at a difficult time in his life, and the Enemy took advantage of the situation.

This dream was a revelation of God's heart on the issue of abortion. He was showing me the state that the world is in where having a baby is considered a burden, an inconvenience, and *an option*. The Enemy of God tries to mask his intentions and make you feel like you are making the right decision because you do not want to mess up your life. All of the things that Mike's friends were talking about in order to convince him to not have the baby were cares of the world. This is an age-old principle. Jesus said

> And the cares of this world, and the deceitfulness of riches, and the lusts of other things entering in, choke the word, and it becomes unfruitful. (Mark 4:19 KJV)

That word for *unfruitful* is the Greek word **akarpos**; it means unfruitful, barren, profitless. The depth of that word is a whole revelation in and of itself.

In the Old Testament, God tells mankind to be fruitful and multiply. That is a *commandment* from God. In this age, we think that being fruitful just means to have a lot of kids, but the truth is that this is a blessing from God and children are a reward from Him.

> Children are a heritage of the LORD: and the fruit of the womb is his reward. (Psalm 127:3)

Similar to the Greek, the Hebrew word for **reward** means compensation, a fare, a reward, a benefit.

In Mark 4:19, Jesus notes that the deceitfulness of riches is something that causes the seed to be choked out. We focus on the Word of God as being the primary principle of the parable of the sower, but in actuality, this parable is about the condition of a person's heart. The good soil is the good heart that is open to receive and nourish the Word of God and allow it to produce a harvest in one's life.

In the dream I had, the Enemy—through his friends—presents to Michael all the cares of the world to try to convince him that, for his own benefit, he should not have children now. They play on money, selfishness, not having a house, etc. All of these take a toll on him, and he just wants to rest. The moment he fell asleep in the dream was when the Enemy took advantage and took him where he wanted without regard for anyone else—including the unborn child.

The kingdom of heaven does not operate according to monetary reward. There is no money in heaven. God is so rich that the roads are paved with gold, and the foundations of buildings are made of precious gemstones. Why would God need money to reward us? The world has corrupted the church's mindset of what is valuable and what is a reward from God. The truth of the matter is that *giving* is what gets you a reward. *Sacrifice* is what gets you a reward. *Being a servant* is what gets you a reward. God does compensate us with money for these actions, but He compensates us with a heavenly yield that is far more valuable than earthly riches.

Children are a reward from God. The Hebrew word for *reward* is **sawkar**, which is a wage that is paid to someone. Since God is not bound to give you money alone as a reward for the work you do, or for the sacrifice you make, He gives you other life-enriching rewards that He Himself says are payment for what you have done in your life.

Think about this: children cause a person to work to provide for them. When you have kids, you give of your time, you give of yourself, you sacrifice sleep, you sacrifice for their sakes, and you become a servant to meet their needs. You would gladly lay your life down for the safety of your children. Then one day, you see the reward of that sacrifice as they become successful, as they contribute to the world, as they bear your grandchildren, as you see them thrive. You are proud of them, and they honor you with their actions. God set it up so that His original command to *be fruitful and multiply* will result in blessings that are innumerable and immeasurable.

Another thing that God revealed to me in the dream was the attitude of the church regarding Michael's unexpected reward from God. The whole dream took place in a church. This church was huge, and it represented the body of Christ as a whole—His church. Michael was kicked out of the church and rejected completely because he was in sin. It is one thing to not let a person lead worship because they messed up, but it is another to completely disregard them in their time of need. Michael's rejection from the church was all it took for him to leave, and in his attempt to do what was right alone, he fell asleep and fell into the hands of the Enemy.

I have seen this happen to people. They take one scripture from the Bible and use it as a means to kick someone out of a church and cut them off from their lives forever.

> Yet I certainly did not mean with the sexually immoral people of this world, or with the covetous, or extortioners, or idolators, since then you would need to go out of the world. (1 Corinthians 5:10 NKJV)

That is not the intention of this verse. At first glance, it may seem like this is the case, but when we read further, we get a different perspective as to what Paul was talking about.

> If anyone has caused grief, he has not so much grieved me as he has grieved all of you to some extent—not to put it too severely. The punishment inflicted on him by the majority is sufficient. Now instead, you ought to forgive and comfort him, so that he will not be overwhelmed by excessive sorrow. I urge you, therefore, to reaffirm your love for him. Another reason I wrote you was to see if you would stand the test and be obedient in everything. Anyone you forgive, I also forgive. And what I have forgiven—if there was anything to forgive—I have forgiven in the sight of Christ for your sake, in order that Satan might not outwit us. For we are not unaware of his schemes. (2 Corinthians 2:5-11)

The only person that Paul specifically told the church at Corinth to cast out was the man that was involved in an incestuous relationship with his father's wife. By law, even if it was his stepmother, that is still incest. Paul shows in 2 Corinthians 2 that the church could discipline someone for a short period of time and still love them. Paul says that the Corinthians ought to forgive and comfort him so he will not be overwhelmed with excessive sorrow. He instructs them to love this man, and he shows in verse 11 that this is to prevent Satan from outwitting us.

The word used for *outwitting* in Greek is **pleonekteo**. This means to covet, overreach, get the better of (someone) by cunning. The use of this word shows that Satan's desire is to have this person so he can gain a victory over him and defeat the church.

How could casting someone out of the church and not showing love to them give Satan a victory over the church? You are doing what was commanded of you, right? Remember, Paul said to do it for a short period of time but to show them love. If you shut them out completely, you (who are supposed to look like Jesus and be a representation of Christ to the world) reject them, and Satan will make them feel as though God has rejected them. Separation from God-fearing Christians allows the Enemy to get into a person's head and creates all kinds of strongholds.

In my dream, Michael was cast out and rejected. I was forbidden to reach out to him, but I still did. I was the only person who tried to help him and encourage him. This resulted in him being given over to the cares of the world and being led off, regardless of his will or the will of those around him. The Enemy does not care whom he hurts. He only cares about fulfilling his agenda, which is to steal, kill, and destroy.

> The thief comes only to steal and kill and destroy. (John 10:10)

God's heart is that we are his children, we are His portion, and we are His inheritance. Like all parents, God has a plan for the life of each one of His kids. He knows what He wants you to grow up to be, to do, and what you will be the very best at in your life.

> For you created my inmost being; you knit me together in my mother's womb. I praise you because I am fearfully and wonderfully made; your works are wonderful, I know that full well. My frame was not hidden from you when I was made in the secret place when I was woven together in the depths of the earth. Your eyes saw my unformed body; all the days ordained for me were written in your book before one of them came to be. (Psalm 139:14-16)

As I wrote this, I heard God's voice very audibly say, "What a sad day it is for Me when I have to write in the book of my children: *Mission Aborted*." This broke me. Be careful when you ask God what His heart is on a topic, because His emotions are much more intense than we can know. It actually grieves the heart of the Holy Spirit, and it grieves the heart of God the Father and Jesus, to have to write in a child's book of life that they never had a chance to fulfill their destiny, whether they would live fourteen days or in the womb nine months, and their plan for this world would be aborted. Or that after they had fought, survived an attempt on their life, and been born alive, they would be allowed to die of exposure because they were unwanted by their mother or a doctor.

Abortion is an antichrist spirit. It works hand in hand with the Jezebel spirit, which attacks the fruit of the vineyard. In 1 Kings 21, we see a physical manifestation of a spiritual attack—an attack on a man named Naboth. The king of the Israel, Ahab, wants Naboth's vineyard. *Naboth* means the *Word of God*. He refuses to give up his fruit to the wicked king, so Jezebel creates a plan to appear like she's doing good but gets others to join her scheme and lies. They manipulate people's hearts so she can kill Naboth (the Word of God) and steal his fruit so it can be devoured by the evil king. This is exactly what lawmakers are trying to do now. Your children are your reward; they are your fruit, and the Enemy wants to devour them. He wants to steal any and every reward that God gives to you.

God's heart is never to bring judgment on a nation unless her people have had every opportunity to repent but instead remain disobedient. God does not want to bring America back to Him by smiting the wicked sinners. That simply is not His heart. If we want to change America and bring the United States back to God's original design for this nation, then we need to start by reforming the body of Christ in this nation. When we begin to pray for our nation and show people the same non-condemning love that saved a prostitute, a tax collector, a salty fisherman, and me and you, then we will see reformation. When we love unconditionally, as God does, then we will see the next great move of God. We will not only see God moving, but we will see an entire generation moving, flowing, and living out the Christian lifestyle that God desires to see in America and in the world.

Chapter 1
The Current State of Abortion, Nationally and Globally

What is the condition of our nation, statistically, since the overturning of Roe v. Wade, and how are other nations involved?

I come to you with the most dire crisis we are facing in our nation today to make you aware of where we are at as Christians. There is a misconception that we can just forget about abortion prevention because Roe v. Wade has been overturned.

The current administration and the FDA have made something more accessible. When Roe v. Wade was overturned, over seventy websites suddenly popped up and allowed the RU486 pill—the chemically induced abortion pill—to be distributed online via telemedicine.

What does this mean?

People are able to log into one of these websites, put in their menstrual cycle, put in their date of birth, and say they want this pill. It costs about $100 at this time. They do not require an ultrasound to verify the date of gestation and how far along these women are in their pregnancies. They are prescribing the abortion pill to women who say their menstrual cycle was ten to twelve weeks, depending on what the site requirement is, since their last menstrual cycle.

That means that a man who wants to force an abortion on a woman can enter the information the site requires. They can put in for a thirteen-year-old the date of birth for an eighteen-year-old. These sites do not verify anyone's identity. They allow women and minors—or whoever is putting in an application for them—to get the abortion pill. It could be someone forcing it upon them. I have seen this at the clinics where I (Brandi) have worked. I have seen men forcing women to get an abortion. The women would run to me, hiding from the man, saying it was not what they wanted, and asking how they could get help. It could be someone who is trying to hide rape or incest, or someone who is underage that just wants an abortion.

What are the ramifications of this?

Think about it. The abortion pill has only been approved for up to ten to twelve weeks as of the latest research per the FDA. If someone put in their menstrual cycle at ten weeks, they were approved for the pill.

But the way they were able to justify doing this without a physician laying eyes on them was because they were getting the pills from pharmacies from other countries.

They put in their information, and these other countries—overseas pharmacies—ship to their house the RU486 pill. It takes about four weeks coming from overseas if there are no delays.

What happens if the abortion pill is taken after ten to twelve weeks?

Let's say a woman who was at ten to twelve weeks is now at fourteen to sixteen weeks, and she takes the pill. She may even be further along than that because she did not have an ultrasound.

The dosage of pills that are prescribed are for a woman who is less than ten to twelve weeks of gestation. In this case, the woman takes a pill that has a lower dose than what is recommended to have a *complete abortion*. She takes the pill and experiences minor bleeding that she thinks is normal because this is what the companies are advertising. Then she walks away thinking the abortion is complete—but it is not.

It is usually enough to kill the baby, but now she has a dead baby in her womb. These women have no physician oversight, so they have no idea this is happening. Within two to three weeks, the woman will end up in the hospital going septic, and she could possibly die because there was a dead baby in her womb. Another thing that could happen is parts of the baby could come out, but not the whole baby.

If, by chance, the whole baby is expelled, these women are typically sitting at home alone in their bathroom—a bathroom they will forever have to go back to multiple times a day. They pass the baby, and then don't know what to do next. Does she pick the baby up? Flush the baby down the toilet? What if the baby gets stuck? Many women go to pregnancy clinics with their baby in a bag and ask what to do with the baby. Then they go back home and live with a lifetime of regret and pain from their decision. Whether they realize it or not, the decision to abort a baby has a forever impact that leads to suicide in 25% of these cases.

In another scenario, a woman takes the pills, the baby is still in there, and the body recognizes it as a foreign object once the baby has passed away. So the body does its job, which is to fight to get rid of the foreign object. The body does this, but the woman is not dilated because of the lack of dosage of medication that was needed. The body then causes a hemorrhage, with massive bleeding, trying to expel the baby that has been killed. The body causes the woman to go into a hemorrhage that can't be stopped without surgery. She may even die in her home.

Now we look at what the current administration and the FDA has put into place. They continue to allow telemedicine, which allows pimps, sex traffickers, etc. to go in and type this information for women. If the women get pregnant, they get the pills, and they give them the pills themselves. They do not have to have eyes laid on them; they do not have to have their identity verified; and they do not have to have an ultrasound to verify gestational age. It is empowering the people who want to have their way with women, their bodies, and their babies.

The current administration has basically said, "We are behind that!" They took this concept and made it legal for physicians who are on telemedicine to write an order. As a nurse, I know a lot of places have standing orders. Doctors are not even present most of the time; they give a standing order to do this, and then the woman takes the prescription to any pharmacy nearby, and the pharmacy has to fulfill it because it has the doctor's signature on it. This is happening in states that have banned abortion because of telemedicine. It is even cheaper now because they have lowered the price from $100 to $20 - $30 for these prescriptions, making them more accessible. Doctors have no idea what is actually going on, but they are prescribing these pills.

Now we talk about abortion rates and hope they have decreased since Roe v. Wade was overturned. I can tell you from our studies that abortion rates have decreased in those thirteen states that have banned abortion. They officially decreased by about 5,000 per state, per month. However, there are still 8,500 abortions that are being performed illegally in these states, and likely more because of telemedicine and women inducing labor using other methods, like seaweed, for example.

Fifty percent of all abortions that occur are considered unsafe abortions, which means they are not performed by medical personnel. So these 8,500 are only the ones happening in states that have already been banned that are *reported*. Think about the other half that are not reported. We can assume that there are 15,000 to 19,000 abortions per state per month in these thirteen states.

In the states that still allow abortion, the current statistics have gone up by approximately 5,000 abortions per state, per month. People who are seeking abortions have now found other methods or they have gone to the states that allow abortions to occur.

I do not want to minimize the celebration of Roe v. Wade being overturned. It was a huge victory for God, for women, for families, and for babies. We celebrate wholeheartedly, but we are not ignorant of the facts and statistics showing what is happening today.

The reason I say this is because I think many in the body of Christ have put abortion on the back burner since Roe v. Wade was overturned, though we still have a crisis going on. I am all about saving every dog I can from euthanasia, but when it comes to babies, how much more should we recognize that they are being slaughtered? They are essentially being sacrificed.

I want to be clear that I am not judging anyone who has had an abortion. If you know me, you know that I will walk through every part of the healing process with you. I will love you, and I will not judge you. Jesus forgave everyone for everything they have done. No one's sin is any worse than mine. Everyone is welcome here, and we want to help you step into your destiny, be healed, and move forward.

But ladies and gentlemen, we need to step up to the plate! Here at Fireside Grace, we have the resources to help these women. We have the resources to help these families choose life. I have personally been a part of saving over 250 babies' lives that I know of. I want to save one million babies. Record it and document it! I want to save *all* the babies; I'm just giving us a goal to shoot for.

This cannot be done with just Robyn and Brandi. We need your help! Seventy of women who choose to get an abortion are Christian. That tells me that my mission field needs to focus on the inside of the church. We have created this guide to abortion prevention and also a post-abortion version, which is very thorough in addressing this epidemic in our world today. We are willing to give this course away for a donation that you feel is appropriate or none at all. We envision webinars where groups of people or friends gather, and we take you through our entire abortion course. We also have it available for individuals that do not have a group.

We need you to step up to the plate and be prepared to minister to someone. The statistic used to be 24% of women in the United States have had an abortion. In 2023, it increased to 29.4%. That means that nearly one third of the women you encounter have had an abortion. There are few who can say that they have never known anyone who has been in that type of a crisis. You have known someone, you could know someone now, and you very likely will know someone in the future. If nothing else, you can be prepared to spread the word and teach others.

Here at Fireside Grace, we exist to make disciples who will do the work of the Father. The Bible is very clear that we need to do good works; in fact, they were prepared for us before we were even born (Ephesians 2:10). So I am calling you to step up and into this position to help save babies. When you save a baby from being aborted, you also save their mother from unimaginable heartache. I have volunteer positions open that I need filled *now*!

There are several roles that volunteers are needed here. For example, we raise up chaplains to be able to serve as crisis responders to situations such as: crisis pregnacies, suicidal ideations, shootings, etc. Our chaplains also serve to answer our hotlines for those needing prayer or resources for an issue. They walk through life as life coaches for those who choose to parent, and so much more.

We will offer free life coaching through the course for the mothers and fathers that choose life instead of an abortion, partnering with pregnancy clinics all over the United States to do this. Pregnancy clinics typically stop following the mother and father after the birth a baby because they do not have the resources for that, but we are saying that we will do that. We want to continue to follow and support them as their child grows.

Yes, it is beautiful when they choose to keep their baby, but raising a baby is hard, and the majority of women who consider having an abortion already have at least one child. To do it all over again when it is unplanned is very difficult. Let's say we had a conversation with a woman and encouraged her and the dad to make the decision to keep the baby. They may come back and blame us for having the conversation that caused them to keep the baby. When it gets hard, a lot of times they feel some regret and take it out as abuse on the baby. We stay connected with them as long as possible to support them and help them realize their value so they can live up to their life's potential. If they know their value, they will know the value of their kids and how to instill it in them.

We do all kinds of things like this, and now we are offering our webinars and information mostly for free. We are asking for your help to get the word out. To say, yes, Roe v. Wade was such a miraculous testimony to the goodness of God and absolutely necessary, but these are the things that are still happening. As Christians, we cannot turn a blind eye to the reality of what is going on in our nation and in our world. There are still millions of babies being aborted per year, globally.

Several states, and even our nation's capital, still offer abortions with no term limit (New Mexico, New Jersey, Alaska, Colorado, and Washington D.C.). Thirteen states still allow abortions from eighteen to twenty-four weeks, and many offer abortions until viable.

Multiple sources show that fifty percent of unintended pregnancies end in abortion annually in countries that restrict abortion. Over thirty million abortions happen behind the scenes, mostly in the lower to middle income countries. About seventy-three million induced abortions take place worldwide each year.

Sixty percent of all unintended pregnancies and thirty percent of all pregnancies end in induced abortion (medical abortion or self-inflicted abortion).

For 2020, California, New Hampshire, and Maryland did not even give the statistics to the CDC.

The Society of Family Planning states the national abortion rate decreased from fourteen per 1,000 women of reproductive age in April to thirteen per thousand in August of 2022. Notably, abortions provided by virtual-only clinics increased from 2,830 in April of 2022 (accounting for three percent of all abortions before the decision) to 3,780 in August of 2022. This shows an increase of 33% in the number of abortions provided by virtual-only services comparing April and August 2022.

The number of abortions that decreased in the states that put a ban on abortions is great, but they are almost the same as the amount that increased in other states, so it pretty much evens out. Overall, there has been a *slight* decline of the number of abortions since Roe v. Wade, and every life is worth that.

It is critically important for us to put pressure on our senators and representatives. I am telling you this as someone who has run for House of Representatives before. They actually take an oath that says they must fight for what the *majority* of their respective community wants. While it is important for us to continue to be politically active, I also see the need for the body of Christ to rise up and be active in our communities.

I know that together we can continue to see a decrease in the number of abortions performed, but there will be major pushback from the pro-choice community. This is already being done. It is already being seen in our current administration with what is being allowed. They are not happy about Roe v. Wade being overturned.

As Christians, we must be useful in this area and not just sit back and say we have the victory. If we do not *maintain* the victory, we will lose it.

The reality is that no one or very few wants to have an abortion. I have met with hundreds of men and women who have considered this for their family, and no one ever wants it. They feel backed into a corner and believe they have to make that choice. But, as the body of Christ, we can step in where the government cannot. We can offer help and support them through the process, so they do not feel obligated to make that choice. When they have hope for their future, more often than not, they will not make that choice.

> For I know the plans I have for you, declares the Lord, plans to prosper you and not to harm you, plans to give you hope and a future. (Jeremiah 29:11)

Chapter 2
Abortion Abolition and Abortion Prevention

I (Brandi) have cried and prayed over this topic. I have carried this burden on my shoulders to get the word out in a way that is respectful, loving, and shows the fruit of the Spirit, but also in a way that gives truth. We are called to administer the truth. With that responsibly and calling comes another responsibility: to be respectful and loving to everyone we speak truth to. That is one reason our ministry is named *Fireside Grace*. We feel called and led to speak about difficult topics that might make people feel like they are in the fire. We make every effort to do it with such grace that every person will feel totally encapsulated in God's love.

That is how we approach the subject of this book. I want to put a disclaimer out there that there will be some very difficult topics talked about here. We cannot say enough on any side of the argument to make everyone happy, but we want everyone to feel respected and know that we are not trying to leave anything out. We may focus on one topic more than others, but we will do our best to cover everything possible.

With regard to the prevention of abortion, I could talk for days about how to minister to women considering it now. I have learned so much about this that I would love to talk to anyone who wants to learn more. That being said, I can also tell you about the bills that are being proposed right now in my area. I can tell you what each of the senators and representatives supports and what they do not, but I see an issue that is bigger than those things. Those are necessary, but we also have to look at the bigger picture. There are issues in our culture that must be reformed in order for our senators and representatives to even consider abolition bills.

The reason I say that is because, as I previously mentioned, senators and representatives take an oath to represent the majority of the community they are representing. If a senator or representative strongly believes something and they are not able to get the backing because their job is to represent the majority, what we need to do is *change the communities* so they can truly represent the majority. It is not a matter of the senator or representative being evil or not.

The hardest part of this topic for me is not getting infuriated with *both* sides of the aisle! A lot of the politicians who say they are pro-life are really pro-choice but don't realize it. They believe in abortion for cases of incest or rape, which is only 0.01 percent of the population that gets pregnant. This is not representing the majority, neither is it pro-life; it is still saying the baby does not have rights because of the situation of the parents.

Again, seventy percent of people who get abortions claim to be Christian, and that number keeps rising because most Christians are afraid they are going to be judged, gossiped about, slandered, and kicked out of the church. They feel ashamed. If you listen to women who considered abortion but decided to parent, most of them will not tell you they were considering to abort. They will say they were unsure about what to do, but the words *abort* or *terminate* very rarely come out of their mouth. Shame comes with that. Shame is not from God, but conviction is. If they truly know it is wrong, they will carry that conviction.

The fact that so many people choosing abortions are Christians is an abomination to the body of Christ. As leaders, we need to stand up and talk about these topics. We need to make sure we are equipping ourselves and our people with pregnancy center information so all the resources these women need can be made available to them by a loving and supportive congregation.

How do we change the mindset of a culture?

This begins by dispelling and debunking the myths and lies that surround abortion in our society. It is not hard to find the source of these myths and lies. They started around 1914 with the women's reproductive rights movement, which, at the time, was loosely associated with feminism and women's rights. However, true feminists and suffragettes did not believe that abortion was right; neither did they believe in birth control. Our society needs reformation to make the necessary changes with the intention of setting it back on track

If any of you know me (Brandi), you know that I was basically raised volunteering in a nursing home! I have writings called *The Wisdom of the Ages*, which are about bringing the wisdom from a few generations ago back into our generation and then seeding it into the next. Those nine years volunteering in the nursing home gave me a good education, and I learned so much from those who had nearly lived a full life. I had the privilege of gleaning wisdom from those men and women who lived and loved and suffered and laughed. They had been through and learned so much in their lives that kids my age did not understand. I have always felt out of place because of that, and I have been drawn more to friends in their fifties and sixties because I grew up hanging out with older people.

There has rarely been a perfect time in history when abortion did not exist. Abortion dates back to the time of Jezebel in the Bible where babies were being sacrificed to their god Molech as worship to Baal. There was not a perfect time to reset society back to, but there was a time where society was following more of the moral standards of the Bible.

I believe those whom I had the opportunity to serve at the nursing home, trusted me. They trusted me to bring reform to our culture and not let it go in the way they were seeing it go. I am working day and night to do that with every fiber of my being. I exhort you to join me!

The purpose of culture, from a biological standpoint, is to maintain conditions that are suitable for growth. A society can represent a collective communal ideology of the time of a person, place, or location. It takes being raised in a certain culture to be sustained for growth. We are influenced by our parents, leaders, and brothers and sisters in our community, as well as our culture.

It is important for us to be very concerned with the culture we are setting for our generation and for future generations. If we are going to step up as Christians, now is the time to do it. What are we doing as Christians to create a culture that is suitable for moral growth in our society?

Ask the Lord to make you a *think tank* so you will consistently think, ponder, and meditate on what you can do for the Lord to reform our culture to bring everlasting change lasting from generation to generation. If we do not make a culture that is suitable for the growth of moral and Christian standards, we will allow that culture without moral standards to rule and reign. When we are killing babies that have already been delivered, we have *completely* lost our moral compass.

I had a word from the Lord the other day in a dream. The Lord said that if we do not rise up and fight this feminist movement, they will have too much power for us to stop them. We must rise up in this hour and learn what we can do.

From a biblical standpoint, wives are to submit to their husbands and husbands are to submit to their wives. It is not wife submit to pastor, wife submit to this person, that person, or anyone who is male. No! The Bible tells us that wives are to submit to their husbands, and husbands, likewise, submit to their wives. Neither of your bodies is your own.

The feminist movement says, "My body, my choice." What about the rights of the child?

Some people use the argument of sentience as a point where life begins and say that is where you should start determining whether or not it is okay to abort. Like Ben Shapiro says, if we say we cannot abort babies after a heartbeat starts, then we should go ahead and kill everyone who has a pacemaker because they have an artificial something outside their body creating a heartbeat. Therefore, they are not sentient. Or for the people who believe brain waves and brain function determine sentience, what about people who are in comas? Are we going to kill them too?

Sentience begins at conception, and I can prove that from a biblical standpoint. The words used for *baby* in the Bible are the same words that are used consistently throughout Scripture from the time of conception and after the baby was born. The words are not different. The Lord sees the baby the same at the time of conception as after birth. If babies in the womb cannot think, then how did John the Baptist respond to feeling the Spirit of God? The Bible says he leaped in his mom's womb when he felt the Lord come in, even though He was in Mary's womb. John leaped for joy! Joy is an emotion. The baby could understand and express joy in the womb. Elizabeth had a super revelation; she knew what was going on with her baby!

Scientists are starting to share research that a mom and baby share thoughts from time to time. For instance, pregnant women will have weird dreams. When this happens, the baby is actually influencing the mom's dreams.

Ben Shapiro talked about a doctor who did not really make the news or headlines, but he aborted a baby at twenty-six weeks. The question was not if it was legal to abort the baby; they wanted to know if it was in the womb or out of the womb. A picture showed the baby fully formed. At twenty-six weeks, most babies born prematurely can survive with the proper care.

The Bible says that unbelievers will actually hate the things of God—not just think they are foolish, but actually hate them. Hating the things of God indicates a struggle with *identity*. To know who you are in Christ is to know who you truly are. If you do not know Christ, you cannot know who you are. These people are always looking for ways to express who they are through feminism, LGBTQ, and every other ungodly expression. Interstingly enough, a very high number of members of the LGBTQ community get abortions. Different studies point to about one fifth of abortions come from people who claim to be part of this community.

We can influence society even as *one* person. Even if we are just one light in a dark room, our light will light up the entire room. What would happen if every one of us affected one person to add their light to the proverbial room?

One thing that we can do to change or reform our culture is, instead of teaching that women can do anything men can do and more, we should teach that it is okay to have differences. It is okay to be weak in one area and rely on someone else to help lift you up. We must collectively begin to celebrate each other's strengths!

At the same time, we must protect our children, our Christian freedoms, and those who do not know the Lord yet. That is what the Lord does. He protects His children, even if they do not love Him yet. Just like your own children: if they ever turned away from you, you would do everything you could to protect them. As Christians, we must also protect the innocent lives that do not know the Lord yet, while creating an atmosphere that will be beneficial for them as they learn to walk with the Lord.

I asked the Lord why we should start with cultural reform, and He said, "We have to water the soil for it to be ready to accept the seed." The seeds in this instance are the bills that are being proposed by activist groups, the words that we plant into women considering abortion, and anything of that nature.

What are issues that need reforming in our society today? We could go through a million of those, but I will focus on the issues that need reform with regard to prepping the atmosphere and prepping the soil to abolish abortion. It is going to take a while to get there. We pray the Lord will make things happen overnight, but just know that if you are taking land little by little, you are doing exactly what the Bible says to do. God doesn't tell us to eat a whole apple at once. By taking land little by little, you will learn to keep your authority and take more land.

> But you will receive power and ability when the Holy Spirit comes upon you; and you will be My witnesses [to tell people about Me] both in Jerusalem and in all Judea, and Samaria, and even to the ends of the earth. (Acts 1:8 AMP)

If you look at Judea and Samaria on a map, you will see that Judea is like a city and Samaria is like a state. Then you go out. You take ground little by little. It was not just random names of cities that God put in that scripture. He specifically showed us to start where we are at and then go out further, and then a little further, and so on.

To do this, there are a number of issues that need reforming in our society today:

- Feminism must be understood and reformed to its original state
- The role of men in society and family needs to be retaught
- The importance of men
- The importance of motherhood
- The importance and value of having a family
- Respect for gender differences (male and female)
- The empowering of both men and women and how we can work together to empower each other
- Belief that the Bible is the moral standard for today
- The church's view of women seeking abortion—eliminating the stigmas and harsh words
- Teaching the truth while giving support
- Teaching abstinence
- Correcting a congregation when abstinence is not being practiced

- Believers involvement in politics and activism

The importance of men in children's lives

I (Robyn) have a son in New York that I do not get to see very often. I want to see him, I try to see him, I reach out, and I pay my child support. I understand that I live in another state, but that would not stop me from flying him out here or getting on Skype to talk with him; I have been prevented from doing these things. I can take his mother to court, but I would have to hire a lawyer I cannot afford. I cannot get one appointed because we make too much money, according to the laws that favor women in court. The legal system makes it very difficult for men to do the right thing. If a woman wants to be stubborn and obstinate, and deny a man his rights, he has to fight in court, but everything is still in her favor, it seems.

The role of a husband and father in a family is significant, and the deficit shows in our society. A high percentage of people who are incarcerated grew up with no father in their home, which caused them to have a litany of issues. They ultimately rebel. When you think about it, they feel like no one provided for them, so now they need to provide for themselves, and they do it how they want to do it.

We need men to step up. Often, women are afraid when the father of their child is considering abortion. When they say they cannot do that, the mother is often forced to raise the child on her own. There must be accountability for men. At some point, men, we need to man up!

Before I was saved, I did not want to pay child support because I thought it was a waste of money. That was the wrong mindset, and men everywhere need to change that. Women should not need to give you a receipt for anything; it is accusatory. Even if the mom went out and bought a pair of shoes, she has the right to look nice and feel nice. If the mom is not depressed, the whole family will be happy. If the woman is depressed because she cannot do anything for herself, that will also affect the whole family.

The whole idea of child support having to be accounted for by the mom is insulting. That kid needs your support and your help, and he or she needs you to be their father. They need you to be there. We need reform to take place that causes fathers to see the value of what they have to offer their children. There are some things that only a dad can teach or impart to a child.

As a woman, I (Brandi) want to share a couple of things that concern me about how women treat men. Obviously this happens in reverse roles as well, but lately, men have been taking some proverbial hits. Some men might be doing things to deserve that, and some women also might be doing things to deserve that. The truth is that everyone deserves a chance.

I see women accusing men: "You're pregnant too. This is your baby inside of me, so you need to straighten your life out too!" But then, in the next sentence, "Well, it's my body, and I'll do what I want." Drop that mindset! Yes, it is your responsibility to take care of your body, especially when it is a host for a growing baby. If you do not want this to be the case, use birth control or be abstinent. If your significant other is not in alignment with birth control, then you need to strongly discuss this before having sex.

Sex before marriage is another subject that needs to be talked about, though there are many married women who are seeking abortions because they feel they do not have the financial support to care for the child. One thing I hear often is, "I've only been able to provide just enough for my kids, so I do not want to bring another one into this scenario."

Another thing that bothers me is that, in the state of Oklahoma, if a man wants to give up his rights to his baby, all he has to do is sign a form. A woman, on the other hand, has to go to court to relinquish her rights. Both parties should be held to the same standard of accountability.

At some point in your life, you are going to want to be a part of that child's life. Babies change a lot of parents—especially first-time parents who have babies and suddenly decide to get their life together. I cannot tell you how many men and women I have ministered to who are ex-felons. They worked hard to get their life together, and now they are excited to show their children the traps to avoid. *People can change.* As long as that is monitored and they are held accountable to staying true to their new identity in Christ, the past is the past. That is awesome! More power to them.

I find it appalling that women can get abortions without the consent of the father. It is unconstitutional and evil to terminate a baby of a father without his knowledge. Here is the thing: there are a lot of women who are afraid that the father of the baby will not be supportive, so they do it without telling him. It is not your right to keep a child—even an unborn child—away from the father, unless it is an abusive situation and the mom and child need protection from him. It is a man's right to know what is going on with his child, even though that child is being hosted in the mother's body.

There are men who are extremely depressed because they lost babies they have always wanted and never got a chance to fight for them. What are we doing for them? The Bible teaches that we are to be *submitted to one another.* That means Robyn's body is mine, and my body is his. We do not make drastic decisions without consulting each other. We are both also submitted to the Lord, so neither of us makes a decision about our body without consulting the Father.

I believe in men, and I believe in women. I believe in allowing a man to open a door for me to show me care and respect. I believe in letting Robyn enjoy the things that I do not enjoy. We pick up the slack for each other in every area because we are a team. When one of us is weak, it is the other's job to be strong. We are stronger together.

My (Robyn) favorite thing about being a man is that I feel respected and valued in our relationship. I do not feel like there is any extraordinary benefit to being a guy, but it satisfies my need or desire to be a leader, provider, and a protector. In the same token, I cook, I clean, I take care of our sons, and I run our ministry behind the scenes. Brandi and I treat each other with respect, and we love each other. Marriage is not give and take; it is give and receive.

Men are naturally physically stronger than women because they are *made* to protect. Men have a tendency to want to protect using physical violence and threats, but I (Robyn) have learned a lot from Brandi about how women respond to things. She is protective and loving by helping me censor what I say and watch.

Men have a vital role to play. Men and women are equally important; feminism has been pushed in our face for so long that too many people are forgetting about respect for men.

We should not look at parenthood as anything less than a privilege. God entrusted our children to us. The Word says that from the foundation of this world, He wrote a book about us before we were even born. He wrote every single page, every single word, and every single detail of each person's life. When God gives you a baby, He says it is a reward. It is also a *privilege* because you are now holding a book in your womb that was authored by the greatest Penman ever! Now you have the privilege of bringing God's kingdom to earth.

To paraphrase, the Bible basically says in Psalm 139: "Before you were formed in your mother's womb, I had a plan for you." There is purpose in *every* life.

We encourage you to ask the Lord what is your role in preventing or abolishing abortion. Just because we abolish it does not mean we will not have to prevent it. When there was a ban on alcohol, people still made and bought alcohol. We need to reform our culture to understand and value the importance of life itself. Just putting laws into place will not achieve that, though they are also necessary. What is the bigger picture here? And what is your place in that bigger picture?

The body of Christ must unify because, together, we are more than enough. We are all in this battle, and Jesus has already won. If He has already won, that means He has already paved a way for us to win. We have to wait on Him and seek His direction.

If you do nothing else, share the gospel with people. If you set people on fire for the Lord, get people saved, renew their passion—whatever they need—that will help to abolish and prevent abortion. You will influence the culture and the mindset of those who love the Lord and are willing to seek and obey His plans and purposes, which are not to abort children.

Holy Spirit, I pray and ask You to manifest Yourself right now to each person reading this and touch them. Let them know that You are there for them. I pray that You would tear down every stronghold, every wall, every lie, and that You would silence and bind every enemy and evil spirit. I shine the light of truth into their life now. Touch their heart and heal them. I pray that in everyone who reads this, seeds will be planted, take root, and grow strong and deep on a great foundation. Raise them up to be strong proponents for abolishing abortion in America. In Jesus's name. Amen.

Chapter 3
Abortion Prevention Crash Course: The Lies Families Believe and How to Counteract Them

In our book, *The Character of Christ,* one of the chapters is called *"Getting Your Needs Met in Christ."* It is very important to operate with good character to be an effective Christian, and to be satisfied, fulfilled, and happy. We also need to know what our needs are, and if we are not getting them met, learn how to accomplish that in healthy ways. This is of utmost importance to preventing abortions because once we know how to meet each others' needs in a healthy way and can help others to get their needs met in Christ, we will be building strong families that understand their identities. Understanding their identities is crucial to placing value on human life, thus preventing abortion.

God created us with emotions. He created our entire being, so He knows that we have needs. He wants those needs to be met. Some of these are:

- Affection: Make me feel like I'm wanted.
- Safety: Allow me to be who I am with all of my flaws, and don't judge me. Give me room to grow and believe the best about me.
- Attention: We all need attention from someone. We need to feel heard and valued. God created that within us.

One thing we need to realize as the body of Christ is that when we—or someone else—have needs that are not getting met, our behavior is typically going to be undesirable.

For example, people who are attacked with the spirit of isolation sometimes come off in undesirable ways. When I (Brandi) was struggling years ago with depression and isolation, I always felt like I needed to have hugs, and I wanted to hang out with people more than normal. I was always the last one to leave places because I wanted to feel that sense of community. I did not want to go back home into isolation at night because I lacked the strength to withstand the spiritual battles I faced when I was alone. That can be overbearing to other people.

Sometimes people will come off as if they are one-upping you in everything they say because they want to feel respected, validated, and be considered smart and worthy of love and belonging. So they will make themselves appear to have knowledge, and in turn, try to make themselves *wanted*. That is what Satan leads them to think they need to do.

If we take a step back and recognize when someone is acting undesirable to us, we can then determine the reason behind it. Typically, when someone exhibits an undesirable behavior, we tend to push them away. That is our natural response when we think they are too much: they are overbearing, codependent, and needy. I get that. Even in our struggles, we cannot suck the life out of people; we must get our life from Jesus.

For example, my three-year-old is going to ask me for milk. He is going to ask me for milk until he can get milk on his own. Later, it will become about relationship. "Hey, Mom, come hang out with me. Let's watch a movie." That comes with time. We are the same with Christians. When we are still learning to get our needs met in Christ, we are constantly asking or seeking subconsciously (or consciously) to get those needs met.

Instead of turning people away who have undesirable ways of getting their needs met, we need to embrace them, press in, and accept them with healthy and strong boundaries. We need to show them their worth by making them feel included and wanted. We can do this by asking them questions, such as: "You know what? I value your opinion. What do you think about this situation?"

How can we meet their needs in such a way that they feel attended to, safe, respected, wanted, and like they belong? These are changes we can make now in the way we love and interact with people.

When I was working as a registered nurse, we had an employee who always made myself and others feel "lesser than" her. The office manager we had at the time had previously (about 15 years before) been accepted into nursing school, and she hoped to become a nurse. She got pregnant and decided the best thing for her and her family would be to drop out of school and go to work. She never did start her career or education in nursing.

Every time an issue came up, she accused the nurses of handling situations wrongly, and I was one of those nurses. At first, I was offended. Then I took it to the Lord and asked Him why I was getting offended. He said, "Because you are insecure also."

The Lord helped me overcome insecurity and feeling like I was not doing my best job. I was treating that patient how the Lord led me and how the book said to treat the patient, but what I really needed to do was validate the office manager's need to feel relevant. She needed to know that her input was valuable because all of our input is valuable.

She was initially very rude to me. She did everything she could to get me fired, but I had favor. She was also a practicing witch, not a Christian. I decided to love the ever-loving daylights out of her! This is *only* possible because of the grace of God.

The Lord led me one day to go into her office and tell her about an issue a patient was dealing with. He said I did not have to take her advice, but that it would turn things around if I went in and asked her how she would handle the situation. It was my license, so it was my decision how I handled it, but I went into her office and explained the situation.

She did not give terrible advice for not having gone through nursing school. I listened to her, I thanked her for the information, and I told her I would let her know how it goes. I took what I could that was safe and helpful for the patient, and I implemented it. I told her the outcome, and I told her every time the patient made an improvement because that made her feel like she made a difference in my life and in the patient's life. It made her feel valuable to our community at work. Of course she was, but I wanted her to feel that even more so. Because I met her need, she became my friend. Did I trust her as far as I could throw her? No. But she was more pleasant to work with! I really believe it helped her feel fulfilled in her everyday life as well.

Sometimes the people that we allow to offend us the most—the ones that we are uncomfortable with or exhibit undesirable behavior—are assignments for us. It is our job as Christians to seek the Lord for how we can help promote them to become who they are in Christ. That is also getting them back to their true identity, which is to be wanted, accepted, believed in, and loved. We impart to them wisdom, knowledge, and understanding. We belong with each other as Christians because, together, we are the body of Christ.

The reason it is so important to recognize that we have needs and get them met in healthy ways is not only because Christ wants us to live fulfilled, but He also wants us to *help each other live fulfilled*. If we are not helping each other become fulfilled in who we are in Christ, we do not value our own lives.

When you know who you are because you know who your God is, you are confident and can overcome any insecurity. We recognize how beautifully we were created. To believe anything different is to dishonor and disagree with the Word of God.

When we get it, and we recognize our worth on this planet, we understand that our time here on earth is very short and that everything we do has a ripple effect that touches everyone we come into contact with. They, in turn, affect everyone they come into contact with, and so on, for generations to come. When we grasp the fact that we are beautifully and wonderfully made, and we believe it for ourselves, then we cannot help but want to share it with everyone else. We will want to see people live up to their fullest potential.

Another issue I find with families considering abortion when they are facing a crisis pregnancy is that *they themselves do not value their own lives*. So how can they see the value in the lives of their children, especially when they are going through a crisis? We can work ahead of time—before families in desperate situations get pregnant—and help each other on a daily basis to live up to the fullest potential we could ever reach. This can be achieved by meeting each other's needs in Christ, going the extra mile to love people who are being difficult, and taking the time to work through difficult situations.

A common example of someone who does not have his or her needs met is someone who has coped by operating in what we call, "Jezebellic tendencies." (For more information on the spirit of Jezebel, see our book, *Expel the Jezebel in Me*.) For example, if someone has a Jezebel spirit and God has placed them in your life as a boss, best friend, pastor, or other position of influence, do not accuse them or call them names. It is your job to help them. Iron sharpens iron. We can say there is a spirit influencing them and that it's a lie from the devil. We can tell them God has a plan for them, Jesus is the door and the way, so He makes a way out for anything that they're going though. For any behavior that Satan is influencing them to operate in, Jesus is the Door and their way of escape. Ask them to talk about it and tell you where it is coming from. When they can identify it, they can flip the script and break the cycle to live a fulfilled life.

I promise you that if someone is operating in a Jezebel spirit, they are not happy about it either. They are in bondage and do not know how to get out of the cycle, or they likely would do it.

Humanity generally seeks good. Uncorrupted people actually set a course toward the good. If we can help others to realize that even when we are at our worst, we are worth fighting for, we will become Christians of such maturity that we will not walk away from difficult people but show them their value.

If just one person believes in you, you can accomplish everything you are called to do. Jesus is that Person. The Holy Spirit is that Person. God the Father is that Person. I will be that person. Do not allow the Enemy to tell you that no one believes in you because that is a lie. You can also believe in yourself because you know who you are in Christ. That is reconciling yourself to the Word of God: coming into agreement with it and choosing to dispel the lies of the devil that go against what the Word says.

We have prayers that we pray, but sometimes our degree of effectiveness in prayer depends on how much we are in agreement with our own prayer. For example, if you pray, "God, I declare I am out of all debt in Jesus's name," how much of your heart is actually in agreement with that prayer? Do you really believe you are out of debt? Do you really believe you are not struggling with it anymore? We have to reconcile our beliefs to the Word of God and who we are in Christ, and what He said has been done, is being done, and will be done. I use this certain example because it is the one that I often hear people say, but they don't act as though they really believe it.

When we value ourselves and help other people get their needs met so they value themselves as well, then we can disciple them. When it comes to an unplanned pregnancy, or what we call a crisis pregnancy (because it is a crisis to the people at the time), they will understand that because they are valuable, the life they carry must also be valuable.

In this ministry, we do not call abortion *murder* or people who have abortions *murderers*. The truth of the matter is, yes, the baby has been killed. That is essentially what happened, but it does no good in the situation to label someone who is in the middle of a pregnancy crisis that way because the Bible says to be angry with someone is basically to murder them. The fact is, our job is to help, support, and love. It is *not* to judge.

Our job as effective ministers (which is all of us) is to approach the situation by binding Satan from influencing the mom, dad, or whoever is involved in the decision-making process, to believe lies that are contrary to the Word of God.

Lies that Satan causes women and men to believe are true reasons to abort

Lie #1: A lack of support

Pregnancy clinics do a fantastic job of supporting women and men who are going through this situation. However, they can only be supportive to a certain degree because you cannot help everyone. An organization or clinic—most of which are donor funded—has to choose what women they are going to support and for what period of time. Most pregnancy clinics are limited in some of their resources because they have to be, or people will not steward well.

For example, at Fireside Grace, we partner with pregnancy clinics that may not be able to continue to support families after they have chosen life and have the baby. A lot of a pregnancy clinic's support is cut off when the baby is born. They support them up until that point, help with education, baby showers, emotional support, love, and financial resources, but when the baby comes, they have to cut the service so they can help they next person going through the same situation. That is the reality, but because I experienced firsthand working in one, I know that their hearts are to help as many women as possible for as long as they can; but they can't do it alone.

One of the ways we support pregnancy clinics (or churches and other groups that are helping women) is to provide free life coaching for couples or single parents who have chosen to keep the baby instead of abort. We continue to support and come alongside pregnancy clinics to help them in every area of life through life coaching and pastoral relationship. In this type of emotionally healthy relationship, we can spiritually coach them into their fullest potential, while continuing to help them with issues that come up with parenting and so forth. Most pregnancy clinics aren't able to provide that, so we are here to meet the need!

This is something that *you* are a part of when you partner with Fireside Grace Ministries. We support single moms in that way by giving them free time and free coaching sessions that would otherwise cost money they need to pay bills. Our supporters help us provide more sessions because the more financial support we have, the more time we have to give to women, and the more people we can train to do this as well.

If you want to start an abortion prevention group or a pregnancy resource center in your church, small group, in your family, or anything like that, we can help you. We will figure out what that would look like and how to do it, and then we would train everyone in proper abortion prevention: how to be the most effective, how to track them statistically, how to follow up, and how to minister to them.

Lie #2: Once they have the baby, no one will be there to help them

I know someone who was facing an unplanned pregnancy. She went to a Christian pregnancy clinic and was given the cheapest diapers possible, which did not hold anything. It was like, "You say you are here to help me, but you give me worthless products." That was her experience.

It is our job to give the best of everything we can. I know the diapers were more helpful than not having any, but as Christians, we should give the best of everything we have—even if it's a box of diapers. Fireside Grace works to block the lie of a lack of support by offering support in the necessary areas. We should *always* go the extra mile. If we cannot provide the support ourselves, we can join with someone else in the body of Christ to help provide what is needed.

If you do not have a ministry but you encounter someone who talks to you about this, ask them how you can support them. The worst thing that can happen is you say no if they ask for something you are unable to give. Or you can tell them you cannot provide that but offer to help them find resources that can. Reach out to us or to Abby Johnson's ministry, local pregnancy clinics, or a local hotline, and they will be able to give you the resources or direct you. Just this can make him or her feel supported.

Lie #3: They have disappointed their parents or spiritual leaders

A high number of those who seek abortions are members of the Christian church. It is very saddening to me because we should be loving people in and through their situations, not making them feel condemned. Condemnation is not your job, and it is not my job. Conviction belongs to the Holy Spirit. Our job is to love each other the way we would want to be loved. There is a time to teach about decision making, and that is prior to someone having a crisis pregnancy. Once she is already pregnant, it is time to make her feel supported.

There are Christian private colleges that will kick you out of school if you get pregnant out of wedlock. A college that you are paying thousands of dollars to attend will kick you out. In my opinion, that is none of their business. They kick people out when they are trying to get a great education for themselves, trying to better their life to do what they feel called to do, and to provide finances for the child they will birth. But no; they kick them out. How loving and effective is that? In fact, it is unbiblical.

We cannot condemn someone who is pregnant out of whatever we believe to be righteous because it has already been done. The time to teach, train, and love like that is *before* they become pregnant. Once that happens, it is too late. And chances are, they feel condemned enough already.

For the majority of people, being pregnant is not fun, especially if it is a crisis unplanned pregnancy for which they can foresee disappointment and shame. Everyone is afraid of shame. Shame says: *You don't belong here anymore because you did this. You are dirty.*

If you are a Christian and you believe in sex only in marriage, and you messed up and got pregnant, Jesus forgives you; He paid the price for your forgiveness too. I guarantee you the person judging someone for getting pregnant has also had to be forgiven of something by Jesus. Once way we can prevent this is also to teach from *The Battlefield of the Mind* by Joyce Meyer, and help others understand that we must learn how to take our thoughts captive and discard the thoughts that are not in alignment with the Word of God. This will help in the process of eliminating decisions about pregnancy, or any crisis, made from a root of people pleasing, doubting that God will provide, and so on.

We have got to get the shame and guilt out of the church. I know several women who have had abortions because they were afraid of what their parents and church would think, say, or do. That is an abomination to Jesus.

Also, on the sub-topic of disappointment, is *racism* in families. If a woman gets pregnant by someone of a different race and her family is racist, this poses some concern to her as well.

We want to love and honor our family, but when we become pregnant (whether you are the male or female), your sole job is to protect your child. That may mean you have to separate or draw certain boundaries for a period of time with your family. It is often hard to do the right thing, but as the church, we must help by teaching how to implement strong boundaries while still showing love and protecting their unborn child.

Lie #4: Lack of housing and other financial concerns

There was a woman who came into the clinic where I was working at the time, and she did not have a home; she lived in her vehicle, which had problems of its own. She already had two children for whom she had given custody rights to her parents because she was already struggling with addiction and self-worth issues. She knew that she was in such a state of depression and mental illness that she would not be able to parent well. She actually made the decision herself to relinquish her rights so her children would be safe while she got help. I personally believe that it required a lot of strength and humility for her to lay down what was most important to her in order to get help and go back to them.

It was at this time that I met her. She was at an all-time low. She had just lost her children, essentially, and she was pregnant again. How in the world would she be able to welcome another child when she could not take care of the ones she already had? This is what she believed. She did not have housing, and this was another child she would lose. It was another person she would fail. She was already in a major state of depression and having suicidal thoughts.

The Holy Spirit told me to tell her that He was going to meet her needs. He was going to give her a home, He was going to give her a better job with better financial means, and He would always supply what she needed.

> And my God shall supply all your needs according to His riches in glory by Christ Jesus.
> (Philippians 4:19)

The verb *shall* actually appears in a verb that we do not have in English. In Greek, however, it refers to ongoing, ever presently getting your needs met in Christ. He has met them, He is meeting them now, and He will still be meeting them tomorrow. It is an ever-present, ongoing verb tense. So *He met, He is meeting,* and *He will meet.*

I told her, "If you really believe in Jesus, and you believe His Word is true, this still resounds true in this situation. He is going to meet your needs, He is meeting your needs, and whether it looks like it or not, He will take care of the baby He gave you."

The Bible says that children are a *gift* to us. They are our *inheritance*. This is a beautiful thing. It is not a burden; it is a gift from heaven. If God gives us the gift of a child, He will give us the means to take care of that child. If we want our children taken care of, how much more does our heavenly Father want to take care of them? He intricately knit them together in the womb and knew them before we ever did Of course He is going to take care of them. The Holy Spirit had me encourage her in this. The two children she had prior were boys. The whole clinic had been praying for revelation, and she felt like she was going to have a girl. It was her deepest heart's desire to have a girl if she ever had another child.

At this time (before the overturn of Row vs. Wade), she was about sixteen weeks pregnant and fast approaching the cut-off time to have an abortion in Oklahoma. She found out the gender right after she made the decision to parent and not abort. It was a girl! She was so glad she made that decision. Not that if it was a boy the baby would be less valuable, but it showed her that she was hearing God. She heard God, and if she heard Him say the baby was a girl and that He made her, why would He not take care of her?

She did keep the baby. We did classes together, teaching her all kinds of parenting topics, and just being her friend. She ended up having a precious baby girl, but not only that, her fiancé got an incredible job. He didn't even have a job when they unexpectedly became pregnant. He made more money at this new job than any job he had before. He actually had a background, so this was a big deal. When she was around six or seven months into the pregnancy, she got a raise at her job and an unexpected promotion, so they were able to get their own apartment!

She was able to complete almost the entire list of things she needed to do to be able to get her other children back so she could have her entire family together under one roof and in her care.

She is one example of many women who find themselves at the lowest of lows, but God always provides. When you step out in faith and trust Him to provide, He will do it. It is not an issue of *if*; it is an issue of *when*.

Always help them to see the bigger picture. When we are in crisis mode, all we see is *now*. We don't typically see what nine months down the road looks like. So much can change for the better in nine months.

Lie #5: They will not be able to finish school

When a woman believes this, she will often think the baby will not have the best life he or she can have. Or she already has a child who is in school, and she is trying to do better for that child, but that child is already *suffering*, according to them, because they do not have the best clothes or toys, or get to go to trampoline parks or other activities.

A nurse I once worked with shared how her mother was unwed in her teens and unexpectedly became pregnant. Her mother was encouraged to abort by the military. But she courageously decided to keep her baby, and she put herself through college, even though it was not easy. She not only made it through but actually retired in her thirties! She ended up being so successful in her career that she was able to retire early and do whatever she wanted with her life. Now, her daughter fights for life too!

We can accomplish what God has called us to accomplish, even when it does not look like we can. That is really hard to see when you are in a crisis. We need to step up and remind people of that.

Lie #6: The world would be better without them

We talk about the importance of meeting each other's needs because depression plays a big role in decision making. If you have ever been in the pit of depression, you know that when you are in that pit, Satan tries to get you to make decisions based on your feelings at that time.

Something common with women who deal with postpartum depression is that Satan tries to get them to believe they should not be their baby's mother—that their kids and their spouse would be better without them. This type of depression leads you to believe the world is better off without you. That is not true. You would not have been created if that were true. It goes against everything the Bible says about who you are in Christ, but I understand because I have been there. That mentality is very dangerous when a woman becomes pregnant or is postpartum, especially for those who do not have a deep-rooted relationship with Christ. Without that, they cannot do the spiritual warfare that will help them overcome those thoughts that lead to bad decision-making and regret.

We need to love one another every day and help each other get our needs met, because we never know what challenges someone is going to face tomorrow. If we can love people where they are at today, it will help them make better decisions tomorrow—even if it is just a smile.

I like to tell the story of when Robyn and I had exposed some very bad things that were going on locally, and we had to leave the state we were in for safety reasons. We moved to another state, and everything was going wrong. I was without a job for eighteen weeks despite putting in numerous applications every few days. It was very unlike me; I'm usually the administer of companies, president of that, etc. This was very hard on me on many levels.

We had a one-year-old at the time, and we were living in an RV that was very hot and miserable—the A/C did not work, and rain would come through the windows. It seemed like nothing was going right, and we had no money for gas or groceries. The Lord always provided, but that was how I felt.

I remember heading back to the RV after going to do laundry, and I just felt defeated. I was hot and tired, and none of us had slept. A guy drove past me when I was on my way back, and he just grinned as big as he could at me for no reason. Honestly, I just started laughing, and then I bawled my eyes out for the next thirty minutes!

At that moment, I realized that one small act of kindness—just a smile—changed my entire week! I was able to breathe when I got back to the RV. I just reset, got the laundry done, and I got a job that week! The Lord kept providing for us. I was able to be an encouragement to our family and not be the one that needed encouragement all the time. I had renewed hope from a person I never saw again. It actually changed my life. It led to me getting a job, which led me to where I was in Tennessee, and it flipped me out of depression and into hope again. That man has no idea he did all that. God will give him credit for that in heaven!

If we do *one* thing that the Lord is leading us to do every day, we may never know the impact we will have on people that will actually get them out of depression. We need to love them to a place of truth so every lie they are believing will be dispelled. And if they are facing an unplanned pregnancy, they will be able to make decisions from a place of hope instead of a place of lack. There are more lies that families believe that lead them to choose or consider having an abortion, but from my personal experience working with men and women in a pregnancy crisis these are the ones that predominately surface. I encourage you to develop relationships with pregnancy centers in your area and ask them what lies they see families believe. This will help you be able to better prevent abortions by dealing with these thoughts in the groups you lead before pregnancies even occur.

Chapter 4
The Role of Single Parenting with Regard to Abortion Rates

Single moms are not just *living off the government*. They are not just having kids to get government checks. I (Brandi) work with women every day, and I have never met a woman that specifically got pregnant so she could get money from the government. That amount of money from the government is not worth what it takes to raise a child. There is a 24/7 commitment to a child that can never be compared to getting a little bit of money from the government. There is so much more to being a mother than that.

Many statistics show that nearly 50% of single mothers get some sort of governmental assistance. One out of three women get child support. So out of all the women who are having babies, only one out of three actually causes the dad to pay child support. It is easy to think, when you see a single mom, that surely they have money because they receive child support. Sometimes women don't want their baby's father to pay child support because they do not want the father to be in the child's life.

About 30% of families with single mothers do not know where their next meal is going to come from. They do not know *if* they are going to eat, *when* they are going to eat, or *where* the next meal will come from. It is not uncommon for a single mother to go hungry so her kids can eat.

A single mother is more likely to live in poverty than a single father who has primary custody of the kids. The father is four times more likely to make at least $40,000 per year. It is an unfair responsibility and burden.

From my experience, only around 70% of single mothers are able to work full time, year-round, and they do not take a vacations or days off because that is not an option for them. They cannot afford it. That still leaves the other 30% in the position of not knowing where their next meal is going to come from.

I (Brandi) have been feeling a call from God for quite a while now to step up and help these women. If we are going to be a ministry that supports women and tries to help prevent abortion, then we need to be a ministry that helps single moms.

There are a lot of single moms between the ages of thirty-five to forty-five who are considered to be in the older range for having young children. They face different challenges as well. I believe they feel less supported because they are not in the position of many younger single moms who still have access and receive help from their parents. These are established adults who face a different set of challenges.

Challenges that single parents face

Loneliness

We have talked with many women who experience loneliness. Even if you are not a single mom and you experience a break up, the loneliness you feel at night can be overwhelming. Can you imagine doing all of the work by yourself, then lying down in bed and trying not to think about the difficulties of carrying the load alone?

I can assure you that nighttime is Satan's favorite time to come after people. Statistically, right before you fall asleep is the time when people struggle the most with being lonely. The best thing you can do is schedule a time for self-care. Make time for yourself; be on guard and ready for spiritual warfare. If you know that you are going to feel lonely at that time, spend time in the Word of God. We all must use our time wisely, but especially single parents. Capitalize on every opportunity to take care of yourself. The best thing you can do is spend time in the Word of God and pray. When you do that, you will not feel so alone. We have a resource for mentally challenging times. We produce "soaking in Scripture" videos to help refocus on the Word and be grounded. These can be found on our YouTube channel, "Tomorrow's Headlines Today," under the playlist entitled "Soaking Scripture."

As Christians, we need to represent Jesus better than we have been. Overall, Christians have not left a very good taste in the mouths of people. For the most part, until now, Christian's have been very fleshly in the way they act and treat people. We have to be able to stand up and help these women when they are struggling and hurting. It is time to step up our game and serve them as we would serve Christ.

> Whoever is kind to the poor lends to the LORD, and he will reward them for what they have done. (Proverbs 19:17)

No one wants to take care of the child

Few people want to volunteer to spend eight to sixteen hours babysitting a child so a single mom can work. So what happens? A single mom works three to four hours when she has child care. But what if the babysitter calls out and cannot make it? The mom calls out and says she cannot come to work because she does not have a babysitter. She is heartbroken because it just cost her $100 she could not afford to lose. When someone is living paycheck to paycheck, losing $100 feels like the end of the world. Then the boss says, "You called in last week because of a babysitter, and you called in twice last month for the same reason. You are going to have to find a new babysitter, or you are going to have to find a new job." She finds herself between a rock and a hard place.

If you are an employer or a teacher, what you can do is ask, "How can I help you?" That is probably the best question you can ask a mom that is struggling. *How can I help you? What can I do to make this easier for you?* If you can make a woman feel supported, then she might not decide to terminate a baby. The number one thing many of these women feel is alone, and that can turn into loneliness and depression.

Depression

There are local counselors—no matter where you are—who help by doing charity work. That could be a way you take care of yourself, but again, spending time in the Word of God is key in fighting depression.

As leaders, pastors, and Christians in general, what can we do to help? What can *you* do to help? Maybe you can offer to take care of their child or offer to buy them groceries. If you really want to invest in a single parent, I think the best thing you can do besides asking how you can help is gather resources for them. Start a GoFundMe account or take some type of an offering to get them caught up with their bills and have $1,000 in savings for an emergency. If a single parent has enough put away for an emergency, it will take away a lot of stress and make their life so much easier. If something goes wrong, they have a cushion.

Jesus told us to clothe people who need to be clothed and feed people who need to be fed. It is not enough to just tell them you are praying for them. Back in the time of the book of Acts, believers would sell their property, their clothing, or anything they had that was of value to meet the needs of the people so no one would go without. They gave whatever they had to help someone else.

One time, my (Robyn) sister did not have money to buy groceries, so I tried to sell my guitar—the only one I had. No one would buy it because it was so old. I prayed about it and went to my pastor because I did not know what else to do. He gave me money to go and buy groceries for my sister so she and her son could eat.

Another time, a friend with three young children did not have money to buy his son's school supplies, clothes, or anything. I bought him shoes, three pairs of pants, six shirts, and all of the necessary school supplies.

Do you know what I got out of it? Nothing. I got my friend's love. They cried because God had just answered their prayers that I did not even know they were praying. Then their kids and friends see it and understand *this is what a Christian acts like.* You are making a difference. When people remember you, you want them to remember you fondly. You want people to remember you as the epitome of Christ.

Do something like that for these parents is like a ray of hope. That goes for anyone, not only a single mom. If you see someone who needs help in any way, stand up for them and their rights, and be there to help them. Be the change you want to see in the church and the world. Each of us needs to rise up and be a leader. Being a leader as a Christian means serving others and meeting their needs.

Another way you can help single parents is to remove the shame and condemnation. It is already hard enough to be a parent. You can feel mom guilt even before you have your baby! Things like, if you ate too much cheese, or if you had too many slices of pizza, you feel bad before you even give birth. Satan tries to take over and turn that into shame and condemnation. You may feel like you are not home enough because you have to work to feed and clothe your child, put a roof over their head, pay for a car, and everything else your family needs. Or maybe you feel like you do not work enough because you have to take care of your child. There is always something that Satan will use to tell you that you are not enough. You can tell him to go back to hell where he came from! You are enough, and you have enough.

The truth is, the Holy Spirit is inside of you, so if you really truly believe you are not enough, then you are saying the Holy Spirit inside of you is not enough.

If you are doing the best you can, God sees that and knows that. That is all that matters. Your child will understand. They're absolutely amazing in so many ways! The cool thing about being a Christian is that we get to offer God to our child. God is the best Father your child could possibly have. Earthly men are absolutely amazing, but when you are raising a child alone, you can rely on Father God to come in and be your Father and a Father to your child.

I remember going somewhere with an ex-girlfriend's son, and someone asked me if he was my son. I said, "He is as long as I am in the picture." As long as I was there, I was going to be a father figure to him. It does not matter whose child it is; you can be a father figure without being in a relationship with a woman. That is the great thing about having your children in church. They get a community that helps you raise them. Even those who are married still need a community to help raise their kids.

You can teach them how to fish, hunt, change the brakes on a car—things I wish my dad had done with me. That will not only make a difference in the child's life, but it will also make a difference in the mom's life because, for some things, a boy just needs a guy to be there. There will always be things that a young man will not want to talk about with his mom.

Most moms I have met just want to know that people care. When it comes down to it, they do not need you to give them the world. Sometimes they just need you to give them your ear, or maybe an extra twenty dollars for groceries, or go to their home while their baby sleeps so they can leave the house for a few hours.

If you are in this type of situation, there are resources available for you. If you are a single mom and struggling, even if it is not a financial need, but maybe emotional, there are groups like *Embrace Grace* all across the nation. This is a support group for single moms which has tons of helpful resources on its website. If you are wanting to help others in need, you can download these resources to have on hand to give out, or consider hosting an Embrace Grace group.

Chapter 5
Current Abortion Types (Medical and Natural) and All About the Reversal Pill

The following information was taken from multiple sources and can be found Online. I have compiled it here for your convenience.

Abortion providers offer both medical and surgical abortions. The types of abortion that may be available depend on factors such as how far along a woman is in her pregnancy and what kinds of procedures that particular abortion provider offers.

Medical Abortions

Medical abortions use drugs instead of surgical instruments to end a pregnancy. For Early Medical Abortion—up to ten weeks from the last menstrual period (LMP)—the abortion pill (mifepristone plus misoprostol) is the most common form of medical abortion. It was approved by the Food & Drug Administration (FDA) for use in women for up to ten weeks after LMP. It is even used beyond ten weeks LMP despite an increasing failure rate. After this, it is done by taking a series of pills that disrupt the embryo's attachment to the uterus and causes uterine cramps, which push the embryo out.

Things to consider:

- Bleeding can be heavy and lasts an average of nine to sixteen days.
- One woman in 100 needs a surgical scraping to stop the bleeding.
- Pregnancies sometimes fail to abort, and this risk increases as pregnancy advances.
- For pregnancies eight weeks LMP and beyond, identifiable body parts may be seen.
- By ten weeks LMP, the developing baby is over one inch in length with clearly recognizable arms, legs, hands, and feet.

Methotrexate is FDA-approved for treating certain cancers and rheumatoid arthritis, but it is also used off-label to treat ectopic pregnancies and to induce abortion. Given by mouth or injection, it works by stopping cell growth, resulting in the death of the embryo.

Medical methods for inducing abortion in the second and third trimester

This procedure induces abortion with drugs to cause labor and delivery of the fetus and placenta. Drugs may be injected into the fetus or the amniotic fluid to stop the baby's heart before starting the procedure to avoid a live birth. There is a risk of heavy bleeding, and the placenta may need to be surgically removed.

Surgical Abortions

Surgical abortions are performed by opening the cervix and passing instruments into the uterus to suction, grasp, pull, and scrape the pregnancy out. The exact procedure is determined by the baby's level of growth.

Aspiration/Suction: Up to thirteen weeks LMP. Most early surgical abortions are performed using this method. Local anesthesia is typically offered to reduce pain. The abortion involves opening the cervix, passing a tube inside the uterus, and attaching it to a suction device which pulls the embryo out.

Dilation and Evacuation: (D&E) – Thirteen weeks LMP and up. Most second-trimester abortions are performed using this method. Local anesthesia, oral or intravenous pain medications, and sedation are commonly used. Besides the need to open the cervix much wider, the main difference between this procedure and a first-trimester abortion is the use of forceps to grasp fetal parts and remove the baby in pieces. D&E is associated with a much higher risk of complication compared to a first-trimester surgical abortion.

D&E after viability, twenty-four weeks LMP and up: This procedure typically takes two to three days and is associated with increased risk to the life and health of the mother. General anesthesia is usually recommended, if available. Drugs may be injected into the fetus or the amniotic fluid to stop the baby's heart before starting the procedure. The cervix is opened wide, the amniotic sac is broken, and forceps are used to dismember the fetus. An intact D&E pulls the fetus out legs first and then crushes the skull in order to remove the fetus in one piece.

What if a woman changes her mind? What can she do?

Sometimes it just doesn't hit you until you are there, and the procedure is about to begin. Many women suddenly realize *I don't want to do this!*

Surgical Abortion

A woman who has decided to have a surgical abortion—whether an early aspiration or a later term D&E—is free to change her mind UP UNTIL the moment the surgical procedure begins. Regardless of whether the cervix softening process has begun, or you've already paid for the procedure, it can still be stopped. It is not too late to stop until there is suction happening inside your uterus. Many women, around 10%, stop the procedure that they were once so determined to have. They're not alone in making this decision.

Medication/Drug Abortion (The Abortion Pill, aka Mifeprex, mifepristone)

At one point, you thought you were certain this is what you wanted. You sat in the clinic and swallowed the first set of pills (mifepristone) that will lead to the end of your pregnancy. You leave the clinic with a bag containing the second set of pills (misoprostol) that are to be taken after twenty-four hours. You were told the pills will cause cramping and bleeding, which will expel the pregnancy.

As you get into your car, you are suddenly filled with dread and regret, and your mind is screaming, "What have I done?!" The good news is that it may not be too late to save your baby from abortion.

The first drug in the abortion pill protocol is called mifepristone. Mifepristone blocks progesterone, which is needed to sustain a growing pregnancy. A new protocol, known as the Abortion Pill Reversal, has been developed that uses natural progesterone to reverse the abortion and rescue the pregnancy. Recent studies have shown a success rate above 60% if the progesterone is started within seventy-two hours of taking the first abortion pill. It may not be too late. For more information, and to find a participating medical professional, call (877) 558-0333 or visit the Abortion Pill Reversal Hotline: www.theabortionpillreversal.com.

There is great information on the Abortion Reversal Pills' website. They answer important questions regarding it's use, how late is too late, etc., and I recommend that every person go through each question on the site so you can educate others about it as well.

Chapter 6
Long-Term Effects of an Abortion of Any Type

One of the most tragic side effects of the loss of a baby's life due to termination (abortion) is the impact it has on the mother. Sometimes we—the body of Christ as a whole—can get so caught up in saving the unborn child that we forget about the humanity of the mother. How often do we truly stop and take the time to ask a mother considering abortion how she is doing mentally?

A woman who is considering terminating her pregnancy is a human being just like you and me. When a woman gets pregnant, it is usually a time of great joy and celebration. People are stoked to be welcoming a new life into their family. However, ten to twenty percent of women, according to Cleveland Clinic Journal of medicine, suffer perinatal or post-natal depression[1]. This statistic is in women who want to have a child. Now imagine how that affects women who do not want to have a child. This can lead to the decision to abort. Without question, abortion takes a catastrophic toll on the health and well-being of the mother.

According to *recent studies*, there is no direct link between abortion and mental health status. However, as we researched this, it became glaringly obvious that this is most likely propaganda to support the narrative that abortion is health care in order to try to help uphold Roe v. Wade.

Government-owned agencies, such as the American Psychological Association (APA), just happened to release new statistics stating they studied X number of women over the past five years, *proving this to be a fact*, just one day before Roe v. Wade was overturned. It is also very suspicious that the APA appears to be the only association that has determined these results, contrary to what several previous studies had discovered globally. Because of these so-called facts, we are going to provide the long-term side effects of abortion according to the majority of reports, rather than just the APA, which is the minority.

In 2018, a study was published by Cambridge Press stating:

> Based on data extracted from twenty-two studies, the results of this meta-analytic review of the abortion and mental health literature indicate quite consistently that abortion is associated with moderate to highly increased risks of psychological problems subsequent to the procedure. The magnitude of effects derived varied based on the comparison group (no abortion, pregnancy delivered, unintended pregnancy delivered) and the type

---

[1]. Review Perinatal Depression: A review, Maureen Sayres Van Niel, MD and Jennifer L. Payne, MD, Cleveland Clinic Journal of Medicine May 2020, 87(5)273-277;DOI https://doi.org/10.3949/ccjm.87a.19054

of problem examined (alcohol use/misuse, marijuana use, anxiety, depression, suicidal behaviors).[2]

Overall, the results revealed that women who had undergone an abortion experienced an 81% increased risk of mental health problems, and nearly 10% of the mental health problems were shown to be directly attributed to abortion.

The most important takeaway is that this statement was published as the result of twenty-two different studies all showing the same or similar data. This same study showed 8.1% suffered anxiety, 8.5% depression, 10.7% alcohol use, 26.5% marijuana use, 20.9% all suicidal behaviors, suicide 34.9%, and displayed that all symptoms were 9.9%.

This study also showed that, after an abortion, there are mental health issues. As a woman gets and abortion, her statistical chance of using a substance to cope with these issues increases significantly. Perhaps the most saddening statistic is that 34.9% of women who have an abortion commit suicide. That means that three out of ten women kill themselves after having an abortion.

When I see this, all I can think is that having an abortion does not just mean one life is lost. There is a 34.9% chance that two lives will be taken as a result of terminating a pregnancy. This study also showed that when a woman births the baby instead, the suicide rate drops by nearly 90%.

These statistics cannot be ignored when we are looking at a woman before us who is considering abortion. You are no longer fighting to save that child alone, but you are fighting to save the mother's life as well. It is imperative that we stop looking at just the baby, but we also look at the woman in her time of need and how the pregnancy is impacting her mental health.

Be mindful of these women. Do not be afraid to make a connection with someone. Love is not just something between a husband and wife, moms and dads and their kids, or whomever. Merriam webster defines love as unselfish, loyal, and benevolent concern for the good of another, such as the fatherly concern of God for humankind; brotherly concern for others.[3]

Next, you must be safe and approachable. It is important to let people know they are safe around us. We do not want to come off as judgmental and condemning. We must be careful about reciting things like, "Abortion is murder" because that is not helpful; it will only make them defensive. People are going to be more likely to approach you for help or seek you for guidance and listen to what you have to say if they feel loved. Remember that Jesus paid the price to save us, and that salvation is through grace. Let that grace be reflected in how you interact with someone facing the difficult decision to terminate a pregnancy. The grace you show a woman in this situation will make her feel loved, which will often draw her into repentance.

There are several other physical side effects associated with having an abortion. According to the National Institute of Health:

---

2. Coleman, P. K. (2018, January 2). *Abortion and mental health: Quantitative synthesis and analysis of research published 1995–2009*. Cambridge.org. Retrieved March 3, 2023, from https://www.cambridge.org/core/journals/the-british-journal-of-psychiatry/article/abortion-and-mental-health-quantitative-synthesis-and-analysis-of-research-published-19952009/E8D556AAE-1C1D2F0F8B060B28BEE6C3D

3. NA, N. N. (2023, January 1). *Definition of Love*. Marriam-Webster. Retrieved March 3, 2023, from https://www.merriam-webster.com/dictionary/love

Roughly one million abortions are performed each year in the United States alone. The total abortion-related complication rate is estimated to be about 2%. Most complications are considered minor such as pain, bleeding, infection, and post-anesthesia complications. Others are major, including uterine atony and subsequent hemorrhage, uterine perforation, injuries to adjacent organs (bladder or bowels), cervical laceration, failed abortion, septic abortion, and disseminated intravascular coagulation. This activity reviews abortion complications and their treatments and emphasizes the interplay between interprofessional team members to minimize the occurrence of abortion complications and optimize management and treatment[4].

From our experience working to prevent abortion, the most common of these side effects is sepsis. This occurs when the baby does not fully deliver (yes, you still have to deliver the baby after an abortion), and parts of the baby are left inside the womb. Those parts can become infected, and if the infection spreads to the blood stream, it can lead to death.

As you can see, abortions do not happen without consequences. These are scientific consequences, not to mention the spiritual ramifications of having an abortion. They are weighty, and we must encourage those to whom we are ministering to think long-term rather than short-term.

---

4. Abortion Complications, Karima R. Sajadi-Ernazarova; Christopher L. Martinez, Affiliations 1 Drexel University College of Medicine

Chapter 7
What the Bible Teaches About an Unborn Child

Let us dive right into Scripture to solidify the biblical proof that a baby is still a baby, whether born or unborn. Go with me to Luke 1:41-44:

> When Elizabeth heard Mary's greeting, the baby leaped in her womb, and Elizabeth was filled with the Holy Spirit. In a loud voice she exclaimed: "Blessed are you among women, and blessed is the child you will bear! But why am I so favored, that the mother of my Lord should come to me? As soon as the sound of your greeting reached my ears, the baby in my womb leaped for joy."

The Greek root word for *baby* in this verse is **brephos**, meaning baby or infant. When we do a word study of **brephos** in the Bible, we find that this word is the same one used to describe a baby that has also been born, such as baby Jesus.

> So they hurried off and found Mary and Joseph, and the baby, who was lying in the manger. (Luke 2:16)

> You formed my inward parts; you knitted me together in my mother's womb. (Psalm 139:13)

The Hebrew word translated as *inward parts* is **kilyah**, which can mean organs, or the deepest parts of a person, such as thoughts and emotions. This verse personifies the unborn child to be able to have thoughts, emotions, and sentience—not just potential sentience, but actual sentience. The verses we looked at in Luke also point out to us that the unborn baby in Elizabeth's womb was able to feel a feeling—joy—and respond to it. Research studies have proven that a baby begins to learn the voice of its mother inside the womb and then remembers it after birth. There is ample proof that babies can do many things in the womb that they will do after birth. Another scripture we can look at together is Gabriel's exhortation to Mary:

> And the angel answered her, "The Holy Spirit will come upon you, and the power of the Most High will overshadow you; therefore the child to be born will be called holy- the Son of God." (Luke 1:35)

This is perhaps one of my (Brandi) favorite verses with regard to the sanctity of human life from conception. If you read the original text closely, you will discover that Jesus had the perfect and pure nature of God from the time of conception. He was referred to as *holy* when He was in Mary's womb—not only *after* He was born. This confirms to us that the importance of each human life begins at conception. Life does not suddenly get more important once the baby is out of the womb. From conception, each person has a plan and a purpose from God, so we must fight to ensure that all babies get the right to life.

Pro-Abortion Arguments for Why Women Should be Allowed to Abort

There are many different arguments as to why those who are pro-abortion say that women should be allowed the choice to abort. We will look at some of these different arguments to equip you with the knowledge and understanding to think about and respond to each individual argument.

A woman should be allowed to abort her baby if the pregnancy is the result of rape

The answer here is no. However, in order to not sound like we do not care for the mother, let us look at a couple of things.

With regard to this law going into effect, the congressman or senator that might present a bill stating such is supposed to represent the *majority* of the district or state where he or she was elected. Therefore, this should not be able to pass into law because the *majority* of abortions are not happening for this reason. In fact, a multitude of studies have proven that out of all abortions that are performed, less than 0.01% are due to this cause.

I understand that statistics can be a little skewed because some women did not feel comfortable to share that truth of the circumstances, but even with those cases added, it is still the minority. There is also ample support for women who do get pregnant through rape. However, since the overturn, more and more women are claiming rape without proof to be able to slip through these laws and get an abortion.

Getting pregnant through rape is abuse, but it also needs to be proven, preferably by either a psychologist or a rape nurse. In each city, there is a team of nurses who are on call 24/7 to come in if someone says they were raped. They will do a complete investigation and submit the findings to the state.

I know a woman who was conceived as a result of rape. Her mother got pregnant with her, and today she is thankful just to be alive and have been given the chance to minister the gospel of Jesus, smell the flowers, taste ice cream, and live life. She would not have gotten the chance to do that if her mother chose to have an abortion because of the circumstances of her pregnancy.

Also, Deuteronomy and Ezekiel both point out:

> Fathers should not be put to death because of their children, nor shall children be put to death because of their fathers. Each one shall be put to death because of his own sin. (Deuteronomy 24:16 ESV)

> The son shall not suffer for the iniquity of the father, nor the father suffer for the iniquity of the son. (Ezekiel 18:20 ESV)

This clarifies things pretty quickly, if you ask me. We must always remember that the mother is scared and often alone, and we should do all we can to support her. We can do this by helping her find resources that offer her free or low-cost counseling for as long as she needs it and is able to receive healing and move on from the trauma of rape. Some ways to do this would to be to find resources in your area that offer this type of a service, or offer to sponsor the payment for a victim of this type of crime. As the church, we are called to surround these women with love and help them prepare for parenthood in any way they need, be it financial support, emotional support, practical support (like throwing her a baby shower), finding her pre- and post-natal classes, help her find adoption resources, etc. Together, we can support women and be an example to the church of how to be of service to people in this situation without them feeling like they have to an abortion.

A woman should be allowed full rights to abortion because the pregnancy is happening within her own body

You may have heard this more popularly as, "My body; my choice." Let's look at Scripture to see what it says regarding this argument.

> Then Jesus said to his disciples, "Whoever wants to be my disciple must deny themselves and take up their cross and follow me. For whoever wants to save their life will lose it, but whoever loses their life for me will find it. What good will it be for someone to gain the whole world, yet forfeit their soul? Or what can anyone give in exchange for their soul?" (Matthew 16:24-26)

One who chooses to live by this motto: "My body; my choice," literally forfeits their soul because they are not laying down their cross. This verse reveals a couple of points. First, taking up our cross to follow Jesus means many things, but with regard to abortion-determined women, it means laying down the reasons they believe they should have an abortion (or be allowed to have an abortion) and following Jesus. We know He does not support abortion. This means laying down our desires and fears to follow His ways. We must be willing to give up everything and live according to His Word.

> Do you not know that your bodies are temples of the Holy Spirit, who is in you, whom you have received from God? You are not your own. (Corinthians 6:19)

When we accept Jesus and lay down our life for him, we become one with Him. This is important because now His will takes precedence above our own. We are to love like Jesus loved—even unto death. While literal, this verse also symbolically means being obedient to His Word and protecting the lives of the innocent, even unto death of our own wants or desires. I have had the honor of helping women overcome the lies of the Enemy.

> On that day you will realize that I am in my Father, and you are in me, and I am in you. (John 14:20)

This is yet another verse solidifying the fact that we are not our own. When we become one with Jesus, we become one with God and one with the Holy Spirit. Just as Jesus remains in the Father, so we are to remain in Him. This is throughout all circumstances or difficult situations that may arise, trusting that He has good plans and a hope for our future (Jeremiah 29:11).

Now we know that these are the values we hold, but we also know what the Bible says:

> The person without the Spirit does not accept the things that come from the Spirit of God but considers them foolishness, and cannot understand them because they are discerned only through the Spirit. (Corinthians 2:14)

So, how do you convince a woman who is not a Christian to uphold these values if she considers them foolish? The answer, in short, is that you cannot. It is not our job to convince; it is our job to live with agape love, the highest and most generous form of love. John tells us the Holy Spirit will bring conviction of sin and of God's righteousness (John 16:8). We must wholeheartedly lean on God's Word and trust that—even when dealing with nonbelievers—He can do anything!

> God can do anything, you know—far more than you could ever imagine or guess, or request in your wildest dreams! He does it not by pushing us around, but by working within us, his spirit deeply and gently within us. (Ephesians 3:20 MSG)

Our job is to trust the Word of God, knowing that He will bring conviction to men and women of His plan, and also enlightenment of the plans of the Enemy. We cannot carry any shame about whether or not the men and women we come in contact with to minister to choose life or death. The Bible says that death and life are in the power of the tongue, and we can help these women choose life for them and their babies by helping them recognize and speak the truth over their situation. The truth is that God will provide all resources necessary to keep and raise these babies because He has already met all of our needs (see Philippians 4:19). Not only has He met all of our needs, but He will continue to do that for the rest of our lives.

Something I (Brandi) consistently find is that if I encourage these women to see the bigger picture, by the time the end of their pregnancy is nearing, their entire life may have changed for the better. God NEVER fails to meet my prayer that these women's lives begin to fall into order. Sometimes we have to help them see the bigger picture because, typically, they are considering abortion based on their current life circumstances. But weeping comes for a night, while joy comes in the morning (Psalm 30:5). Each day is a new opportunity for something good to happen for every one of these women, and we can exhort them to be able to see that! While this may be hard for us to grasp as Christians, the Lord will use us to give them hope while He is compassionately wooing them to Himself.

In summary, we are one with Christ. We have laid down our individuality to become one with Him, including all of the choices we will make from this moment forward. *My body; my choice* becomes *Temple of the Holy Spirit; His will*. These values will get some pushback from those who are not Christians, but we must not forget that, from my experience, over 70% of women seeking the abortion option state that they are Christians. If they are blinded to the truth in Scripture, we have been given all authority in Scripture to heal the blind and set them free. We have also been given authority to teach women to speak the pros (life) over having a baby instead of focusing on the cons. Always remember, you have everything you need within you to minister effectively to any woman who is considering aborting her pregnancy. You've got this. Be as bold as lions and gentle as doves. We believe in you!

Chapter 8
Scripture Arguments People Use to Defend Abortion Rights

There are people who claim to be Christians but also believe they have found scriptures to support abortion. Let's look at one of those portions of Scripture to see what it says in the original text. We will look at the story of Tamar in Genesis 38:

The story of Tamar

When Tamar was told, "Your father-in-law is on his way to Timnah to shear his sheep," she took off her widow's clothes, covered herself with a veil to disguise herself, and then sat down at the entrance to Enaim, which is on the road to Timnah. For she saw that, though Shelah had now grown up, she had not been given to him as his wife.

When Judah saw her, he thought she was a prostitute, for she had covered her face. Not realizing that she was his daughter-in-law, he went over to her by the roadside and said, "Come now, let me sleep with you."

"And what will you give me to sleep with you?" she asked.

"I'll send you a young goat from my flock," he said.

"Will you give me something as a pledge until you send it?" she asked.

He said, "What pledge should I give you?"

"Your seal and its cord, and the staff in your hand," she answered. So he gave them to her and slept with her, and she became pregnant by him. After she left, she took off her veil and put on her widow's clothes again.

Meanwhile Judah sent the young goat by his friend the Adullamite in order to get his pledge back from the woman, but he did not find her. He asked the men who lived there, "Where is the shrine prostitute who was beside the road at Enaim?"

"There hasn't been any shrine prostitute here," they said.

So he went back to Judah and said, "I didn't find her. Besides, the men who lived there said, 'There hasn't been any shrine prostitute here.'"

Then Judah said, "Let her keep what she has, or we will become a laughingstock. After all, I did send her this young goat, but you didn't find her."

About three months later Judah was told, "Your daughter-in-law Tamar is guilty of prostitution, and as a result she is now pregnant."

Judah said, "Bring her out and have her burned to death!"

As she was being brought out, she sent a message to her father-in-law. "I am pregnant by the man who owns these," she said. And she added, "See if you recognize whose seal and cord and staff these are."

Judah recognized them and said, "She is more righteous than I, since I wouldn't give her to my son Shelah." And he did not sleep with her again. (Genesis 38:13-26)

There are those who believe this example in the Bible actually teaches that in the instance where there is prostitution, the baby should be aborted as a command of God. Tamar was the wife of Er. Er was wicked in the sight of the Lord, and God killed him. Then Onan was betrothed to Tamar. He was spilling his seed on the ground during sex and was found to be wicked in the sight of the Lord. God killed him as well. The reason Onan did that was because he knew that if Tamar did not have children, he would be the next in line to receive the double portion of inheritance as the first-born son since his brother Er had passed away.

Long story short, Judah slept with Tamar while she was disguised as a prostitute, and he impregnated her. He did not know this was the case and found out that Tamar was pregnant and accused of being a prostitute. He said to burn her. Tamar was the daughter of Shem. It was Judah's prerogative as a judge over the land to burn her; *not* a command of God. Some people say it was God's judgment for her, even though this was Judah's law and not God's. Later on, when the mosaic law was given, it was declared a sin for the daughter of a priest to become a temple prostitute.

In light of this information, we can see that Judah did not want her killed because she was pregnant, but because she was assumed to be guilty of harlotry. He was sentencing Tamar because she was accused of being a prostitute.

We see this same thing happening in Hosea:

> I will not punish your daughters when they turn to prostitution, nor your daughters-in-law when they commit adultery, because the men themselves consort with harlots and sacrifice with shrine prostitutes— a people without understanding will come to ruin! (Hosea 4:14)

The author of the argument above declares that Hosea is saying that God is allowing the murder of children in the following verse:

> Give them, O Lord—What will You give? Give them a miscarrying womb and dry breasts! (Hosea 9:14)

At face value, that seems to be very barbaric of God, but it is actually a ray of hope. I say that because this particular verse is referencing the end of days when the antichrist is in power. When reading Scripture, we need to read it in the proper context.

> What will you do in the appointed day, And the day of the feast of the LORD? (Hosea 9:5)

This appointed day is referring to the end of days, and the feast that is mentioned is the feast at the festival of the harvest.

Jesus likens the end of days to a harvest where God sends out his angels (Matthew 13:39 and Revelation 14:15). Some argue that Isaiah 7:20 describes how and who will carry out the supposed punishment; however, that verse is referring to a time after Jesus has come to the world already (see Revelation 14:13-17).

Then they flip back to 2 Kings, which is a time before Jesus was born. The reason it is important to know that the verse referenced is an end-time verse is because we can identify that those killing babies (as in all cases where the Bible references the ripping up of babies) are not Israeli, not Christian, and not God-fearing men.

The fact that this is an end-time verse allows us to refer to Isaiah 13:5-18. In these verses, you will see references to the weapons of God's wrath or indignation coming from the farthest reaches of the heavens. Later, in verse 9, it describes these times as the "day of the LORD." Isaiah then goes further to explain the exact events of the end of days and what these *Medes* will be doing in those days. This all ties into why it will be a blessing for women to not have babies in these times.

The people that are stirred up in these times are wicked and vile.

> Their infants will be dashed to pieces before their eyes; their houses will be looted and their wives violated. See, I will stir up against them the Medes, who do not care for silver and have no delight in gold. Their bows will strike down the young men; they will have no mercy on infants, nor will they look with compassion on children. (Isaiah 13:16-18)

The argument further states that Numbers 5 declares that God will perform an abortion Himself if someone is found guilty of adultery. Knowing the nature of God, I do not believe this is the case at all. Also, we do not see that happening in our world today. In fact, when Scripture states the woman's belly will bloat and her thighs will rot, It certainly sounds like it is referring to pregnancy, but it is not. There is no mention of the child or of the woman being pregnant.

> Then the priest shall put the woman under the oath of the curse, and he shall say to the woman—"the LORD make you a curse and an oath among your people, when the LORD makes your thigh rot and your belly swell." (Numbers 5:21)

The Hebrew translation of *thigh rot* is **yarekek napelet**. Translated into English, this says *your loins fall*.

The Hebrew translation of *belly swell* is **bitnek sabah**, which means *your womb swell*. This is describing a pelvic organ prolapse. Dr. Kevin W. Windam states:

Pelvic organ prolapse (POP) can cause problems with pelvic pressure, pelvic pain, pain with intercourse or problems with emptying your bowel or bladder. If these problems become more severe, this can cause chronic pain conditions as well as lack of intimacy. Also, patients with chronic constipation can have problems with bloating, abdominal distention and pain. Lastly, patients with an inability to empty their bladder due to POP can possibly have recurrent bladder infections and/or kidney infections and possibly even kidney failure[5].

As a result of being found guilty of sin, not by any man but by God, her uterus would prolapse. Something that I would like to point out is that this entire ordeal was the result of a husband becoming demonically possessed by a spirit of jealousy.

> If a spirit of jealousy comes over him and he is jealous of his wife when she has defiled herself, or if a spirit of jealousy comes over him and he is jealous of his wife when she has not defiled herself. (Numbers 5:14)

Notice it does not say an angel of jealousy; it says a spirit of jealousy. I surmise that the spirit that tempted the woman to commit adultery was probably the same one at work in the husband who was accusing her of adultery, which incidentally would result in the stoning to death of the adulterer.

Now, let's cover the author's view on Exodus where they declare the Levitical law only regards a baby as property and not as a human life.

> If men fight, and hurt a woman with child, so that she gives birth prematurely, yet no harm follows, he shall surely be punished accordingly as the woman's husband imposes on him; and he shall pay as the judges determine. But if any harm follows, then you shall give life for life, eye for eye, tooth for tooth, hand for hand, foot for foot, burn for burn, wound for wound, stripe for stripe. (Exodus 21:22-25)

First of all, *nowhere* does this state that the unborn child is property. The verse she is referencing is verse 21, which refers to the unjust and unfair treatment of slaves. Verses 22-25 refer to the premature birth and possible harm or death of a child in its mother's womb. Then whatever harm was caused to the baby will be done to the man who harmed the child and the mother.

God cares about every child, whether born or unborn. Let's be thankful that God does not hold us to the standard of the law that He gave the Israelites because anyone who coerced a mother to abort a baby would be guilty of murder. They would be required to be killed or maimed depending on whether or not the baby survived or was wounded forever as a result of the process. That is sobering to think about and a strong exhortation to protect unborn babies.

---

5. Hartford Healthcare: https://hartfordhealthcare.org/services/urology-kidney/patient-education/pelvic-organ-prolapse

Chapter 9
Waves of Feminism and Rape Culture: Why They are Important

What are the waves of feminism? There are apparently four waves of feminism. Right now, we are in the third and fourth. These last waves of feminism are very ambiguous as to which one is which because the differences are those on social media, which is now the prevalent vehicle of influence. It has brought up the old term *patriarchy*, but in the early 1900s, there was what was called *first-wave feminism*. In the 1960s, until the eighties or so, there was second-wave feminism. Then in the nineties, there was third-wave feminism. And now there is fourth-wave feminism. They kind of blend together, so the years are kind of gray because they move into different waves that we will look at in this chapter.

What I (Brandi) have noticed from studying this is that it usually becomes a new wave of feminism when the original pioneer, or handful of pioneers of the predecessor of each new wave, passes away, and then it gets picked up by someone else. The torch gets passed to the next generation who have their own struggles they want to deal with. It just keeps being passed on and passed on, almost like a generational issue gets passed on.

I do want to start out by mentioning that Susan B. Anthony was one of the first among the women to stand up for women's rights. I am not talking about how you can walk around naked. I am talking about equal pay, equal jobs, equal opportunity for education, etc. I agree with Susan B. Anthony that women should make just as much as men if we have just as much training in a field and if we are as qualified or more than a man in the same position. For example, if you have more training, and we are competing for the same job, then you should make more than me. That is how capitalism works. That is how the business world works. Whoever has the most experience in dedicating their heart to the job gets the most pay. It seems pretty simple to me, but that is second-wave feminism. Susan B. Anthony was more of a suffragette. She wanted voting rights, but yes, they were all working to advance women's rights. Like I said, most of it carries over from one generation to the next, and they pick up where the previous left off, essentially.

The first wave of feminism really started in the late eighteen hundreds in America, Norway, England, and a few other places. Primarily, what it was in America—and this is the type of feminism that we are talking about here—was women getting the right to vote, equal rights, to be treated like they were actually a human being who could own property, and so forth. Also, some of the subsection ideologies of first-wave feminism were reproductive rights. People like Margaret Sanger and others emerged who believed in so-called reproductive rights for women. This is where modern-day abortion stems from.

I actually read an article online that said there was a drug that people used to give women who were raped before abortion was legal. It would cause the fetus to die of liver failure in the womb and was used in India and other countries. Some still do it today.

Reproductive Rights

Margaret Sanger was pretty notable for founding Planned Parenthood, and she championed this cause before the phrase *reproductive rights* was coined. The basic premise is that it is a woman's right to decide when she wants to have a baby, if she wants to have sex before marriage or sex for recreation, or if she wants to abort a fetus. It says that a woman has the right to choose because it is her body. Her choice, right? Well, it is also a right to be safe—the right to use birth control or not, the right to good quality health care, and the right to education including STDs, menstrual health, and protection from practices such as genital mutilation.

The reproductive rights movement began to develop as part of the human rights movement under the United Nations in 1968. There is a whole lot more to that, but to summarize, it concerns women's sexual, gynecological, and mental health issues. They were not a priority until then, and since then, the United States has supposedly been incorporating those.

I am very well informed, and I feel very well cared for as a woman. As a matter of fact, I am a reproductive women's health nurse, an educated woman who is also a business owner, and a wife and mom who believes in submitting to my husband. I do believe that we have access to good health care now, and I am thankful for the people that fought for us to have that. I am very well educated; all you need to be educated now is the ability to read and access to the internet, which a lot of places have for free now. You can google whatever you want to learn about your menstrual cycle. I promise you will find it. You have access to physicians. You can even get government insurance if you qualify. I am not really sure what else anyone could want.

Something came up the other day; I was listening to a discussion between women talking about the right to birth control, and that it should be free. Well, someone has to make it. People need to be hired to do that. There have to be solutions and solvents, many types of ingredients, equipment—a full-fledged manufacturing plant is needed to make birth control. Nothing in life is free. Nothing comes free except the love of Jesus.

I also saw something circulating around Facebook that said that one-third of millennials and an even higher percentage of Gen Z think socialism is a good idea. I am a millennial, and I know that Socialism is very dangerous. We hear how in Sweden and Canada, for example, socialists are doing awesome. What they fail to understand is that because things such as health care are free, it is hard to get good health care. Because it is not privatized, there is no competition.

The premise of socialism is, *I want to be equal with everybody else. I want a free education, free health care, free this, and free that*. The idea is not wrong, but the mindset is unhealthy. This mindset has more to do with a sense of entitlement than compassion for others. No one has figured out a system that works and benefits everyone, but if all the *free stuff* comes at the cost of our *freedom*, the price is too high. What we are trying to do is start a cultural reformation to bring about cultural change. One thing that must change is this mindset that everything should be free, everything should be handed to me, everything should be given to me, etc. Of course these women want free birth control. They do not understand that they will pay for it one way or another.

As ministers, this is something we deal with frequently. We give away a lot of material because, to us, it is important. God always rewards us for it. We do not charge for the gospel, but what we charge for is our time, effort, and cost of making CDs and creating books and courses into recordings. My full-time income comes through ministry, but what a lot of people do not understand is that we still have to pay to create. You do not just walk into a bookstore someplace and walk out with a $99.00 exhaustive concordance study Bible for free, right? It costs money to make it. And yes, we have to pay our bills just like everyone else.

Abortion was largely pushed in the early 1900s as a means of genocide for the sake of eugenics and selective reproduction, which are not okay. It is not okay to choose who has a right to live and who does not. If you want to talk about human rights, then let's talk about human rights. Margaret Sanger specifically wanted a form of genocide to remove black people, people in poverty, and those with dissident disabilities or impairments. I know many people who have disabilities or impairments in my own family. They deserve the same right to life, and they are an absolute joy to be around. Their weakness actually becomes their strength, and my life would be so different without them. They love life. They are not upset; they are thankful to have the chance to live.

It is not the right of any human to determine whether someone else gets to live or die. You determine that when you determine to have sex. There are consequences for every action and inaction; there is no other way to put that. We have birth control. Now we have other contraceptive methods. We have family planning where we know all about how to track our cycles and not have sex five or six days leading up to ovulation and a few days afterward. That is science. It is not hard to wait a few extra days to have sex. And if it is, then maybe you should evaluate why you are having sex.

Sex is not part of a healthy relationship outside of marriage. It has actually been proven to reduce the quality of relationships. There are a few different statistics which prove that women specifically have a much more fulfilling sex life when it is in a marriage covenant. Imagine that. When you partake as husband and wife, you value it more. Waiting shows that you think the other person is worth it. You will find more on this in the next chapter!

Rape Culture

This is a sensitive subject, and we do not want to hurt or offend anyone, but one thing that we do want to talk about is the fact that neither men nor women should hypersexualize anyone. I (Brandi) know that is a word that has determined feminism, and that is fair. I will say that not everyone is out to rape you. If you think that, you probably need counseling because of trauma. I do not say that offensively; I am saying that seriously. If you fear that people are just out to rape you, we would love to mentor you through that.

Men, you do have a responsibility to be *sober minded* and to *take your thoughts captive,* as do women. I get hit on by women just as much as I do by men, even with a ring on my finger, because there is little respect and no boundaries in the culture that we are living in right now. I find that there are a lot more women that sexualize me than men in their mind. Men do it, too, but my point is that we have to protect each other. To say that we should teach men not to sexualize women, well, then women, why are you focusing on intentionally building your glutes? I promise you it is not just so you can stay healthy and have muscle weight. It is so you can look good for men or for women. That is sexualizing your body.

There may be some who are working their glutes and their hips and trying to get that tiny waist for themselves, but the majority of it is for people to look at you. Do you know how I know that? Because then everyone shows it off. You cannot look at social media without seeing it. You would be surprised how many people we have blocked or unfollowed from our Facebook because we do not like to see women strutting their stuff online. That goes for men too, so there is no double standard for us here.

I know this is a difficult topic, and it will probably rile up some feathers. I unfollowed somebody just the other day because every single picture was them working out, flexing their muscles, shirtless, and all this stuff. It is not because I am overweight and jealous. No, that is not the case. It is inappropriate and unholy. It is one thing to share your accomplishments, but I do not need to see a picture of you without your shirt to do that.

Men must learn how to control themselves, and women must not lead men into temptation—or vice versa. We are to protect one another. I got this revelation, and God said, "You are not against having a beer, but you would not have a beer with someone that you know has a problem." No, I will not because we are not to lead others down a road of temptation. Women, it is not about you. If you think that you can show your body and express who you are by means of what you wear, and if what you wear reveals more than is appropriate, then you need to learn how to express who you are a little better. *You are more than your body.* That is what you are preaching, and it is what you are saying, but it is not what you are demonstrating.

Men, we need to treat women with respect—treat them like we value them and don't want anything in return. We could have a platonic relationship and just be a safe person for them if they ever need help. What if we conducted ourselves with actual respect? What if we taught our sons that? If we treat women with the same reverence as the Bible says: treat younger women as though they were our sisters, and treat older women as though they were our mothers, then our culture would change.

I (Robyn) remember listening to Shawn Bolz say that when he was young, he found out that there were magazines with provocative pictures of women. He asked his dad if he knew about them, and his dad said he did, but he did not look at them. Shawn asked him why, and his dad asked him, "How would you feel if that was your mom or if that was your sister, and you saw that?"

Shawn said he would not like that at all. So his dad said, "Well, that is someone's mom, that is someone's daughter, that is someone's sister, that someone's best friend who went through that." So what if we taught our kids to ask themselves how they would treat someone if they were their family member?

I had good relationships with women before I was married, as just friends, because we did not have sex. Some of them still want to have conversations, but it is not appropriate in the same way anymore because I am married. They knew that I was not sexualizing them. I also knew that their number one complaint most of the time was that Christian men would come on to them and make sexual advances toward them. It is actually a high number in the church and something that needs to change.

What I want to see is men treating women with respect and as friends rather than sexual objects. Don't be snooping through their pictures, trying to see if there is something inappropriate or sneak a peek at their cleavage if she is not your wife. Chances are, unless you are already engaged, you might not marry that person—likely if you date around, and especially if you have intercourse before marriage. It says in the Bible to focus on what is *right* and *good* and *pure*.

It is not okay to get drunk

In addition to this being a command in the Bible, it is unwise because it can put you in a vulnerable position. High anxiety is considered an addiction, and biblically, it means *not sober minded* or *having an irrational fear*. We understand that there are people who struggle with those issues. If you know anything about us, you know that we are here to help them and love them through it.

When you are at a party and you are drinking, men should not take advantage of you. But what if they are drinking and they are not in their right mind either? If you are showing everything, wearing basically nothing, and they are touching you, it will likely lead to intercourse. As women, we must keep away from situations that could become dangerous, and we must keep our friends safe as well.

Men are terrified of this because they do not know if a woman will wake up the next day and cry rape. I do not mean that to be a joke because I have very personal experience with similar things. We cannot put ourselves in a position where we are not in control of our body; the moment that we do, we subject ourselves to things that are harmful. That is not right for the man, and it is not right for the woman.

Alcoholic beverages are called spirits. They can induce you and open you up to evil spirits. People even hallucinate and do hallucinogenic drugs to open their mind to be able to interact with the spirit realm, with their spirit guide, with their spirit husbands and wives, etc.

Do you know what the government taxes? Alcohol, tobacco, soft drinks, fast food, sugar, gambling, and pornography. Do you know what they call that tax? The *sin tax*. Here is the thing: We are not calling you sinners; we are just pointing out that it is contrary to the Word of God. Our government really does not try to obey God at all in most cases, and even they call it a sin tax.

We cannot talk about these things without talking about a certain term, and I apologize to anyone it offends, but it is a term that is out there right now. This fourth wave of feminism—and a little bit in the third wave—has brought about the popular term coined *slut shaming*. This is the concept and idea that a woman is a slut who wears revealing clothing because they claim that we objectify everything.

People with this point of view say that conservative women who talk about their virginity as something pure—something to keep for their husband—is nonsense. They believe you do not lose anything; they believe that when you start having sex, you gain something. Virginity is a very real thing. This is not a concept; it is a prominent issue in our society. The only way to combat this is to pray against principalities and raise our children right with father and mother both taking an active role in the family, setting the example and expectations.

A generation has emerged that believes purity is not important, and that if you claim to be pure, somehow you are shaming and condemning people who do not wait until marriage to have sex. Well, first of all, if you feel condemnation, that is something in you. We could be proud to be a virgin and not condemn anyone, or we could call them a slut. We should *not* be calling people sluts, but it is a real thing. We should see others through the eyes of Jesus. Jesus would never call someone a slut, though He would tell them to go and sin no more.

We should not shame or condemn anyone. At the same time, you cannot take my stance on virginity, flip it, and say that I am controlling, shaming, and condemning you for having sex outside of marriage. Now, if you are convicted by the Bible that says to remain pure until marriage, then that conviction is yours, and it is for your benefit. It has nothing to do with how I live my life. I live my life in accordance with how the Holy Spirit leads me to live in obedience to the Word of God.

The Bible tells us that those who are unsaved will hate the values, traditions, and morals of the Word of God. It says they will consider them foolish, so we would be foolish to expect them to understand our values.

We should not condemn or shame them, but we cannot let them change our identity in Christ or cause us to not be obedient to the Word of God. And nothing they say should change our love for them.

I will not stop talking about how virginity is the best thing to do until marriage. Just because culture tells me that I am condemning by saying otherwise, that is not my motive. The voices of culture will always twist the Word of God and the words we speak. I am not even trying to convict anyone because that is the Holy Spirit's job. I am just trying to relay the many benefits of saving yourself for marriage. Let me tell you one of them: My husband trusts me immeasurably. Also, guess what? No STDs, no unplanned pregnancies, and a whole lot less heartbreak.

The other thing that happens when you have sex is that you get soul ties with every person you sleep with. Whether you were aware or not, you have emotional ties to those people that need to be broken. They are demons. Every time you have sex with someone, all of the demons that person has are given free access to your body because you are essentially saying, *I become one with you*. Sex is more than just a physical act; it is a spiritual act that has severe consequences when done outside of marriage.

There is an evangelist named John Ramirez who was active in the occult and high-ranking in satanism. He was the third highest satanist in New York City until he got saved. One of the things he said he used to do is sleep with women while possessed by a demon so he could transfer his demons into her. If you choose to ignore this, that is your choice. The truth is out there, and the truth is what sets you free.

Many women are in horrible situations, and I know it cannot be easy. It is not easy if you have been molested or raped. It is not easy if you have needs that you are looking for someone to fulfill in your life. That is where Jesus comes in and where you have to learn to develop a personal relationship with Him. I promise you that you can be strong enough to not have sex outside of marriage, and we can teach you and help you find that strength. Yes, I do mean *strong*, because it is easy to have sex outside of marriage.

Many women measure strength by how many men they can control and get to sleep with them. That is a Jezebel spirit in the sense of control, but really it is *weakness*. It is easy to sleep with men. Just look around you, and you will find a man who wants sex. It is not hard. The thing that is always harder is taking the high road.

I love these women. I take care of these families all the time. I love them, no matter what situation they are in. My desire is to see less heartache in them. With regard to why I do not wear revealing clothing, I believe that once you get married, your body becomes your husband's, and his body becomes yours. My body belongs to Robyn, and his body belongs to me. I want to maintain it for him. I find it very attractive that I am the only person that sleeps with my husband and vice versa. I trust him. So many women I encounter today—I would say about 85% of them—say that they are unsure if their spouse is sleeping with other people or not. That's not okay!

If you are a young female reading this, and you are wondering about open relationships and venturing into other things, girl, it is not worth it! Don't do it; it is a trap. You never know what could be going on in other people's minds, behind their lives, or the infections in their bodies. Birth control does not always prevent pregnancy, and it cannot be counted on to prevent diseases from spreading.

Once you are pregnant, it is not your right to choose to terminate another person's life. You deserve to be surrounded and loved by everyone in your community, especially Christians, because you will need help. You will raise your child and go through counseling and whatever else you need. The DNA of a child from the moment of conception is different from your DNA. Therefore, it is not your right, your body, or your choice. If a baby is a whole separate human being from the moment of conception, My body; my choice is not a valid argument for abortion.

The whole idea of birth control and reproductive rights actually originated with Margaret Sanger. You can look her up; do your own research, but here is one of the things that she asked, and it is something that is widely circulated among people who are pro-choice:

> What if the baby's gonna be born sick or have a mental defect or be born deformed?

Here is where that demonic idea came from, and I'm just gonna call it what it is—it is *demonic*. It is dehumanizing a human life so you can justify killing it, just like the Nazis did in the 1940s. Here is what Margaret Sanger said:

> I think the greatest sin in the world is bringing children into the world that have diseases from their parents that have no chance in the world to be a human.

She thought that if babies was born sick, diseased, or defective, they should not have the chance to live a human life. She and her cohorts considered them to be less than human—unfit and undesirable. But that is not up to her, like that is not up to any human. She said that we are all created equal, right? Isn't that the whole premise of feminism? But she also said:

> No chance in the world to be a human being, practically delinquent prisoners. All sorts of things were just marked when they were born.

This is her reasoning for aborting a fetus. Remember she said, "That is the greatest sin people can commit."

Another thing she said is:

> The most urgent problem today is how to limit and discourage the over-fertility of the mentally and physically defective.

This means to discourage people she considered mentally or physically defective from having babies. That is the source of where this argument came from.

A bill that was recently introduced would require men to have vasectomies after having three children. Where are the men's rights? If we talk about feminism, we have to talk about men's rights also. The premise for this is because there is no limitation on men's reproductive rights. Actually, it is legal to forcibly sterilize a person against their will in thirty-one states plus Washington D.C. This goes back to the early to mid-1900s!

Saying that abortion is a restriction of women is wrong. It is completely ignorant of the fact that there is different DNA of a different life inside of a woman that begins at the moment of conception. Most people who are not in the body of Christ cannot understand this, but these are some of the things we have to pray about when we encounter unbelievers. How do we love them through their difficult life situations? How do we protect ourselves? Men, you have got to put on some rose lenses and put your blinders on so you only focus on loving women with the mind of Christ. It is the same for women. We should not objectify each other. I want to look good for my husband. We are built with the natural desire to do that for someone. But if this is not inside of a marriage, and protected so only your spouse sees it, then it can get really dangerous.

We personally do not believe in the use of birth control, but I worked at a clinic where I give out birth control. Most women who do not want to wait until marriage to have sex do want to prevent getting pregnant. I support women, and even though I don't believe birth control is God's plan, I still support women who choose to use it. I help them get things of that nature, because in those situations, the use of birth control could be an abortion prevented. We must fight the battles in front of us right now. If loving these women means providing them birth control, then let's do that. We will love them into salvation and committing their life to Christ.

Robyn was married and divorced, and he lived that kind of lifestyle for a little while before recommitting himself to the Lord. Even so, I considered him a virgin. Did you know that research shows that after seven years, your body is completely full of different cells than it had the previous seven years? It shows that a female's hymen actually can grow back after seven years. Once again, you would truly by medical definition be a new man or woman. If you are struggling with this, don't be ashamed. Don't be afraid to reach out because we know how to help you. We know that these are very real issues—real people with real struggles. We are here for you. We are not against you; in fact, we are not against anyone. But it is time for the body of Christ to rise up and start talking about these topics Today is the day, because one day, it may be forbidden for us to discuss these things in public. And remember, this ties into the importance of getting their needs met in Christ (see chapter 3).

Chapter 10
Understanding the Biblical Argument for Purity

"Your capacity to say no determines your capacity to say yes to greater things."
-E. Stanley Jones

When I (Brandi) was twelve, I had the amazing opportunity to attend an event called *The Silver Ring Thing*. The conference was fun, the leaders were loving, and I was very vulnerable at the time. However, little did I know that the theme of the meeting was abstinence.

Abstinence; no one wanted to talk about that. Yet, there we were, adolescents in a huge church, talking about sex. It was actually refreshing! There were so many different views, stresses, and pressures being placed on me at the time about sex, that I was just thankful someone in authority would discuss the topic and bring some clarity to my hormonal brain!

Abstinence is the reckoning to refrain from all sexual activities until marriage. Now, you may be reading this and saying, "Well, that is not for me; I am already sexually active." However, secondary virginity can have the same effects as being a virgin originally, so keep reading!

Let me preface this by saying that no matter what, *you are loved*. I am not writing this to point out sin, to condemn, or to do anything else along those lines. I am writing this because we keep finding that some have never heard of abstinence, and we want to get this topic out there so each individual has a chance to make an even more informed decision about his/her sexual integrity.

You might be asking, "You mean, if I have had sex already, I can become a virgin again?" The answer is actually yes! God is a God of grace, so why wouldn't there be another chance to redeem sexual integrity in our life? This is called secondary virginity. Actually, common in Hebraic culture is the belief that after seven years of abstinence, one does become a virgin again because it is said that after seven years, a female's hymen becomes once again intact. There are second chances! And let me tell you something: I am married to someone who was in a previous marriage but then became abstinent for seven years. We thoroughly enjoy the benefits of it, and I considered him a virgin when we got married. Yes, I was a virgin because I believed the truth about what I will further write. Stay tuned!

It is not easy to abstain once one has been introduced to sex, and it can even become an addiction that some have to fight to overcome. However, you can do it if that is what you want! However, it will not be accomplished by might or will, but by the empowerment of the Holy Spirit.

Why teach on abstinence?

I am going to go into researcher mode for a minute, so hang in there with me. Abstinence is the only way to fully protect yourself from STDs. No contraceptive pill, condoms, implants, etc. offer 100% protection.

Those who are sexually active before marriage have higher incidences of:

- Attempted suicide
- Abuse
- Depression
- Unplanned pregnancies
- Contracting sexually transmitted diseases that can leave long-lasting effects and even cause infertility

Those who wait to engage in sexual activity until marriage are proven to have:

- Greater self-esteem
- More fulfilling sex
- Longer happier marriages

When I (Robyn) got saved, I became celibate. I determined that I was not going to have sex until I got married, period. That was seven years. I did not look at porn. I did not look at women inappropriately or lust after them. I was not gonna talk to anyone or do anything at all, because I am a Christian and the Bible says that we are supposed to be *pure*. That is hard in the church because there were times when I would get into a relationship with someone, and I would test the waters. I would tell her, "I absolutely will not have sex before marriage." Probably more than half of my relationships ended because their response to me was, "I don't know about that." I would say, "Well then, I don't know about you!" Then I would break up with them or they would break up with me because they did not think the relationship would work out. They were right; and I would silently ask God to help me end it in a loving way, without being a jerk. I was not going to be unequally yoked. Because I waited, I got the best woman in the world. I love her, I value her, and I cherish her.

And guess what? We did not have to find out if we were sexually compatible. I have heard that concern from people in the church many times. *How do you know if you are sexually compatible if you do not have sex before marriage?* That is not how sex was intended to be. It was intended to be where we submit to one another equally. We learned how to work together to please each other in working communication. If you are not willing to submit and help each other in the ways that make each other happy, then I do not know how much more compatible you could be. I think *compatible* is a selfish term because the real issue is this: What if I want something and she doesn't? Or vice versa? Marriage is about *compromise*.

Marriages that are built with the couple having sex for the first time within a marriage prove to have better trust throughout the marriage. Spouses who wait for sex as a gift for each other in marriage typically feel more safe, special, and valued, and they walk in a stronger sense of identity within the marriage. Spouses do not feel as strongly that they have to meet an ungodly or unfair expectation in the marriage bed, and they can learn the boundaries of sex together for what they believe is okay and what is not okay. The list of benefits goes on, but for all intents and purposes, I will stop there.

If you are fighting the good fight of abstinence at this time, let me (Brandi) give you some pointers that Robyn and I found to keep us on the right path. First of all, we are proud of you. Sometimes you just need to hear that from someone who is fighting, or has fought, the same battle. You are in good company, and you are never alone. When I was not married, Satan fed me every lie he could to tempt me to give in. For example, he told me, "You are missing out!" This was one of the main lies I heard constantly. Then one day, the Holy Spirit told me in a still small voice:

> *"Brandi, I am good. I am good to the core, and I am always good. I am also the God of abundance. If I am always good and give in abundance, then do you really think I would be withholding something truly good from you? No. I would be the first to give it to you. I have set the boundary of no sex before marriage to protect you. You are going to have to trust Me on this one."*

Then, I remembered that Satan is the father of lies. So if he was telling me that I was missing out, then I really wasn't because Satan cannot tell the truth; he only tells lies. That helped me a lot; though I had to repeat out loud and in my mind the truth to that lie many times, I held on to that revelation.

Second, Satan would tell me that I was not being a serving significant other and that I was not meeting my partner's needs at the time, so I could expect that he would eventually cheat on me. This one was very hard for me to overcome. It took a long time for me to process that this was a lie from Satan and not the truth because I love to serve and meet the needs of my significant other.

I am going to pause right here and tell you this: sex is not a need that needs to be met outside of a marriage bed. If it was, we would have been instructed that it was okay for it to be met before marriage. God clearly outlines the boundary of not having sex before marriage, and He would not keep us from getting a need met. Therefore, giving your significant other sexual intimacy is not meeting a need. It is participating with them in coming into agreement with the Enemy's plan for their life and your life. If they decide they need sex to be in a relationship, then they are not in unity with your beliefs about the Bible.

The Bible clearly tells us to only enter into a covenant agreement with someone who is in unity with our biblical beliefs. If they are not, or at least at that time, they are not the right one for you. Third, Satan tries to convince the unmarried that sex is necessary to develop intimacy. However, sex is an expression of the intimacy that already exists within the boundaries of marriage.

Read this eye-opening quote by Alice Fryling, in an article titled, "Why Wait for Sex?"

> Genital sex is an expression of intimacy, not the means to intimacy. True intimacy springs from verbal and emotional communion. True intimacy is built on a commitment to honesty, love, and freedom. True intimacy is not primarily a sexual encounter. Intimacy, in fact, has almost nothing to do with our sex organs. A prostitute may expose her body, but her relationships are hardly intimate[6].

What was it that ultimately helped me remain a virgin until marriage? I will tell you that it all boiled down to this: I was madly in love with Jesus Christ! I made Jesus my priority because He made me His priority, and I wanted nothing more than to obey Him. This obedience was not fear-based, and I think that

---

6. https:/studentsoulintervarsity.org/why-wait, Alice Fryling 20

is the main difference between myself and some of my friends who also accepted the challenge and call to abstinence. The majority of my friends who accepted that call and committed to it eventually gave in and broke the commitment they made to God, their future spouses, and themselves. The main difference I have observed through the years is that those friends that gave in all had one main thing in common: they were *obeying* God out of fear or because they were told it was the right thing to do. I wanted, and still want, to obey Him out of love because of the love I have received from Him. Most of these friends of mine had head knowledge of God but not experiential heart knowledge of Him.

If you are someone who has head knowledge of God and you want experiential, heart knowledge of Him, please join me in praying this prayer right now:

> *Jesus, please let me experience with my senses the vast amount of love You have for me. I believe I will receive these experiences from You and with You. Thank You. Amen.*

Where does the Bible say not to be sexually active before marriage?

While there are several scriptures on the topic, I love simplicity, so I will provide one and then let you reach out to ask for more or do a person study on it. Robyn and I love teaching on this topic because of the weight of the revelation we have personally received from this scripture and how it changed our fight to remain pure. Take a look at what Paul said to the Corinthian church:

> Or do you not know that the unrighteous will not inherit the kingdom of God? Do not be deceived: neither the sexually immoral, nor idolaters, nor adulterers, nor men who practice homosexuality. (1 Corinthians 6:9)

The term, *sexually immoral*, found in the verse above, is Strong's concordance number 4205 and means *fornicator* (one who partakes in sexual activity before marriage) and **pornos** (short for taking part in pornography). This verse clarifies that no one is to partake in porn or fornication. It also clarifies that pornography is adultery and is just as much sin as actually having sex outside of marriage. The Bible later describes that **pornea**, **pornos**, or pornography is not okay within marriage either. That, however, is a separate topic than what is being written about here. Please contact us for more information about how to get free from pornography or the truth about porn in the Bible. We know the struggle is real, but it can be overcome!

We are beckoning you today to choose this day abstinence and keep it as unto the Lord. He has a better plan for you than you could ever imagine. We are here to support you, and we are here to help guide you through that, whether or not you have had sex before. We are here to also be your accountability partners. Robyn ministers to men regarding this topic, and I minister to women.

My motto has always been that if one person will take the time to believe in you and walk through life with you, you can accomplish everything you want to in life—and more. We are here with you and for you, and we believe in you. Help us change the world by becoming the change, one person at a time.

One of the things that kept me abstinent through the toughest times was the fact that I had signed an agreement to remain pure until marriage, and I strongly believe that if I sign a contract, I must be a person of integrity and uphold that to which my signature is written. Please email us at firesidegrace@yahoo.com, and we will send you a contract to sign committing to not having sex before marriage. This contract will have a spot for another person to sign as well who witnesses you make this commitment. This should be someone who will commit to supporting you while you fight the good fight of purity. We, of course, will commit to being there for you during the good and bad times as well. Anyone who signs this contract gets a free life-coaching class with either Robyn or Brandi, depending upon your gender. We value and believe in you.

Jesus said that if you look at someone with lust, you commit adultery. I am not trying to condemn anyone; I am trying to make a point. I read a scripture earlier that said that if a woman has sex with someone who is betrothed to another and she is not married, it is still considered adultery.

Once we become Christians, we commit our bodies and our lives to Jesus through a covenant, and we become His bride. We are the bride of Christ.

I (Robyn) remember asking God what He thought about this, and He said, "Just because they are not married now doesn't mean they are not somebody's wife." God is not God if He is limited by time. He is not limited by anything except restrictions that He put on Himself because He is righteous and just. He wants us to be able to depend on Him.

You will not die if you don't have sex. Sex is not a need outside of marriage. It is a need inside marriage because Jesus said not to withhold it from each other. However, outside of marriage, sex is not a need. He tells us that He will meet all of our needs.

Again, we are not to enter into marital relations with someone who is not 100% on board with the Bible. That is one of the reasons that I (Brandi) broke up with my ex-boyfriend ten years ago. I gave him plenty of time to choose the Lord's ways or not. He was not pressuring me to have sex at any time, and I am thankful for that. I think he was a good man for that, but he was not in agreement with me that you should remain a virgin until marriage.

It should not be said, "How do we know if we are sexually compatible?" This is the wrong question because, once you are married, you both lay down your life for each other. As long as it is within the healthy boundaries that God has set up inside of marriage—without porn or anything like that—you have the conviction that God is giving you and His blessing. I want to do what it takes to meet my husband's needs, and he will do what it takes to meet my needs. That is what you do. You sacrifice for each other and get good at meeting each other's needs because you are married and you love each other. You committed your bodies to each other and your whole heart. You are going to make sacrifices for each other. That is what marriage is. The whole compatible-before-marriage thing is a lie from Satan.

Because porn is fornication, in a sense it means that when you look at porn, you are actually prostituting yourself. You are selling yourself out to the devil. You are selling yourself back into bondage and slavery. People who are not saved yet are still in bondage, but the principle remains true. You need to understand that watching porn is prostituting yourself. That is what it is. Your body is not yours to prostitute. Pornography is a type of idol worship.

You cannot give your body away as a Christian; you already committed it to Jesus. This is the time in the body of Christ we have to be all in. We do not want any lukewarm believers. Otherwise, stop saying that you are a Christian.

I (Brandi) was always taught to honor my word, and while there have been times that I failed, I have worked very hard and steadfastly to make sure that I honor my covenant. To me, a signed agreement is a covenant. I was presented when I was a teenager with an abstinence agreement. I signed it, and that helped keep me pure until marriage. Every time I thought about going back on my word, I remembered the document I signed.

We want to bring a Millennial and Gen Z standpoint with a Christian perspective to these issues we are facing today, rather than beat around the bush. We have to speak the Word of God because this generation is not hearing it.

Chapter 11
Birth Control: A Cultural Controversy

In the eyes of many Christians, birth control is a touchy topic. It has created significant controversy among believers because there is often a connotation of sexual immorality, promiscuity, or fornication associated with it. Many believe that birth control is a violation of God's law and should be condemned as such. Let's get to the root of all of this, shall we?

Let's begin with the origin of the term *birth control*. Birth control is defined as the control of the number of children or offspring born, especially by preventing or lessening the frequency of conception: contraception: contraceptive devices or preparations[7].

This is a term that was coined by the infamous Margaret Sanger in 1914. The idea of birth control was to give women the ability to choose when to have kids and how many kids they would have. Her ulterior motives were more devious than simply giving women the right to choose when to reproduce. To the contrary, most conservative views at the time believed that having such contraceptives (birth control) available would lead to greater immorality among women.

Margaret Sanger is well known for her research in Eugenics. Eugenics is the practice or advocacy of controlled selective breeding of human populations (as by sterilization) to improve the population's genetic composition[8].

Sanger believed that she could create a better human race by weeding out those she deemed undesirable, or in one term she used, *human weeds*. Her infamous quote was this:

> How are we to breed a race of human thoroughbreds unless we follow the same plan? We must make this country into a garden of children instead of a disorderly back lot overrun with human weeds.

In her writing, *The Eugenic Value of Birth Control Propaganda: 1921*, Sanger writes:

> In the limited space of the present paper, I have time only to touch upon some of the fundamental convictions that form the basis of our BIRTH CONTROL propaganda, and which, as I think you must agree, indicate that the campaign for BIRTH CONTROL is

---

7. "Birth control." Merriam-Webster.com Dictionary, Merriam-Webster, https://www.merriam-webster.com/dictionary/birth%20control. Accessed 6 Oct. 2024.
8. "Eugenics." Merriam-Webster.com Dictionary, https://www.merriam-webster.com/dictionary/eugenics. Accessed 6 Oct. 2024.

not merely of eugenic value, but is practically identical in ideal with the final aims of Eugenics."

As we can see, in Sanger's own words, birth control was part of her eugenics ideology. In Sanger's mind, birth control was the most viable end-all-be-all to accomplishing her goal of weeding out undesirable humans. In fact, in the very same article, Sanger states:

> As an advocate of BIRTH CONTROL, I wish to take advantage of the present opportunity to point out that the unbalance between the birth rate of the "unfit" and the "fit," admittedly the greatest present menace to civilization, can never be rectified by the inauguration of a cradle competition between these two classes. In this matter, the example of the inferior classes, the fertility of the feeble-minded, the mentally defective, the poverty-stricken classes, should not be held up for emulation to the mentally and physically fit though less fertile parents of the educated and well-to-do classes. On the contrary, the most urgent problem today is how to limit and discourage the over fertility of the mentally and physically defective.

Make no mistake, birth control was not just a means to give women power over their own bodies. It was not to allow families to choose when they would or would not have children. It was a means of preventing the spread of undesirable social classes as Sanger states in her own words.

Now that we have gotten to the crux of what birth control is and why it is so controversial, let's get back to the idea that contraceptives (birth control) were believed to increase sexual immorality among women. Let's establish what sexual immorality is. The Bible uses the word **porneia,** in Greek, to describe sexual immorality. This is directly where we get the word *porn* from in English. Strong's defines it as harlotry, idolatry, or fornication. Merriam-Webster defines fornication as consensual intercourse between two persons not married to each other. Therefore, we can determine that the biblical definition of sexual immorality is directly correlated to sex before marriage.

If you google the question, *do contraceptives increase sexual immorality?*, you will find that the typical propaganda in support of the liberal viewpoint appears. However, just dig deeper and look at the research for yourself. In a study done by the National Institute of Health, they observed that sexual concurrency and contraceptive use among young adult women did increase when they were having sex and how many times they had sex when using a contraceptive (birth control) of some sort. The study stated:

Contraception is measured weekly with dichotomous indicators of whether respondents used any form of contraception, used condoms specifically, used a hormonal method, and used condoms every time they had sex in a given week (if at all).

Respondents used contraception in 80% of the weeks they had sex. They used condoms specifically in 45% of weeks when they had sex and used contraception[9].

Comparatively, another study showed that 90% of women who were using birth control were having sex.

---

9. https://www.ncbi.nlm.nih.gov/pmc/articles/PMC6450760/table/T1/

We see from these studies that using contraceptives does actually increase the amount of sex a person has with one or more partners. We also see from these studies that people who use some form of contraceptive are indeed more likely to have sex as a result.

This may or may not come as a surprise to you, but the church today does not seem to share the same mindset about contraception that our forefathers had only a century ago. Approximately 99% of all Christians have used or currently use contraceptives. It does not seem to be much of an issue at all except in certain denominations.

The reason for this is the belief that using contraception to control the number of kids you have puts you in the place of God, so you are deciding how many kids you have and when. Many associate it with the sin of Onan:

> Then Judah said to Onan, "Sleep with your brother's wife and fulfill your duty to her as a brother-in-law to raise up offspring for your brother." But Onan knew that the child would not be his; so whenever he slept with his brother's wife, he spilled his semen on the ground to keep from providing offspring for his brother. What he did was wicked in the LORD's sight; so the LORD put him to death also. (Genesis 38:8-10)

In God's eyes, intentionally doing something to prevent the conception of a child was a sin worthy of death.

The Bible says in Psalm 127 that children are the reward of God. It likens children to a wage that God entrusts us with. To deny God the ability to bless us with children is essentially robbing ourselves of a divine blessing from Him. However, there is no express law that forbids a Christian from using contraceptives.

Since there is no express law or rule that says birth control is forbidden by God, it becomes a matter of moral judgment. If your conscience forbids you from taking birth control and it seems a sin to you, then it is a sin for you. That does not mean we then have the right to try to force other people to believe the same way that we believe.

When we are ministering to a person, it is imperative to remember that not everyone is a Christian. That means that not everyone has the same standards that we have, nor do they answer to our God. They may worship their own god, be their own god, or choose not to believe in anything.

If you are in a position where you are asked for advice for the best contraceptive, a good place to start is by offering purity. The safest form of birth control is to not have sex. However, many people will not accept that as an answer. According to several studies, 80% of the church has sex outside of marriage, and 88% of the world has sex outside of marriage. Many Christians that you will offer purity to may not receive it. At this point, it is best for us to consider other safe alternatives.

There are sixteen different types of birth control that can be grouped into six different categories: ovulation prevention; fertilization prevention; barrier methods; natural methods; surgical methods; and emergency contraception.

An example of an emergency contraceptive is the Plan B pill. The Plan B pill works by taking it within 72 hours from the time of possible conception. It is increasingly gaining support within the culture of unprotected sex. It inhibits the implantation of an egg by altering the interior lining of the uterus. This prevents a fertilized egg from attaching to the uterine wall and causes the newly conceived child to be rejected by the body.

Some may mistake the birth control pill for the Plan B pill. These are not the same. Plan B causes the uterus to reject a newly fertilized egg, whereas the birth control pill prevents an egg from ever getting fertilized at all. Birth control pills thicken the cervical mucus, and they also thin down the lining of the endometrium. All of this is designed to slow down an egg's journey and prevent it from becoming fertilized. This is not an abortion pill. Abortion is the termination of an already existent pregnancy, whereas birth control is the prevention of the egg from ever becoming a viable fetus.

Make sure that you meet the person you are ministering to where they are at. Be careful to not judge those who don't believe what you believe. Simply offer them the best choice you can that will help prevent them from taking a baby's life and endangering their own health.

Recently, studies have shown that different types of birth control in various forms increase the likelihood of getting some form of cancer. For example, the risk of getting breast cancer increases by up to 44% for women taking hormonal birth control.

The risk of breast cancer increases for women taking oral contraceptives. One statistic shows that women taking oral contraceptives increase their risk for breast cancer by 24% in those currently taking the contraceptive, and a 7% increase for those who had taken it at some point in life.

In 2017, a significant prospective study from Denmark found that newer formulations of oral contraceptives were linked to breast cancer risks. Women currently using or who had recently ceased using combined hormone contraceptives experienced a drastic increase in breast cancer risk of about 20% compared to those who had never used them. This risk varied to a whopping 60% increase in getting cancer, depending on the specific type of contraceptive, and it also increased with longer duration of use.

Let's talk about the risk of cervical cancer. Women who have taken oral contraceptives for five or more years face a higher risk of cervical cancer compared to those who have never used them. The risk of cancer drastically increases coinciding with the duration of use: one study showed a 10% increase for less than five years of use, and a stunningly high increase of 60% for women using oral contraceptives for five to nine years, and a doubling of the risk for ten years or more. However, the risk of cervical cancer decreases over time after women discontinue oral contraceptive use.

This brings us back to the best form of birth control, and that is not having sex. The more sexual partners a person has, the higher the risk (male or female) they have of developing cancer. Certain studies show that men who have had 10 or more sexual partners are 70% more likely to get cancer than those having sex with 0 or 1 partners.

Studies also show that women having 10 or more sexual partners have a 91% increased risk of developing cancer.

These numbers are too high for anyone!

Chapter 12
The Biblical View of Adoption

We have discussed the various lies that women believe as to why they need to have an abortion and how to minister to them to help them feel supported enough to choose life. However, there are times that they will not choose to parent and that is out of our control. There is good news though! We can introduce them to creating an adoption plan and teach them what that would look like.

There are many barriers when it comes to introducing the topic of adoption. For example, a mother may immediately say, "If I'm going to carry it and do all that work, I'm not going to give it away." Sadly, this is very commonly seen in practice at women's clinics and pregnancy resource centers. However, if the mother is willing to listen, we can still continue to point out the positives of the adoption option and plant the seeds of it for her to consider.

One positive is that she will not have to live with the regret of taking a life. The British Journal of Psychiatry published a study stating that women who had an abortion were at an 81% increased risk of having a mental health issue. Women who had an abortion were also found to be 34% more likely to develop an anxiety disorder, 37% more likely to experience depression, and 60% more likely to attempt suicide[10].

Most women think that adoptions are still what are called, "closed adoptions," where you don't get to know the parents that chose your baby, and you don't get to be involved in the child's life. Today, there are many, "open adoption" agencies, and this is great news to share. Most of these agencies will have the parents that are seeking to adopt create fun portfolios for the mothers of the babies to go through, and they get to be involved in choosing the new parents. They also get to determine how often they see or talk to the baby, all the way up until he/she turns eighteen. Sometimes it helps to share an encouraging adoption story you know of and how that baby changed the life of the new parents forever.

For obvious reasons, it is also very important that the mother knows that most agencies are at no cost to her and will cover her healthcare bills during her pregnancy and birth. Something else we like to point out is that later in life, when the parents of children are gone, all they have left sometimes is their siblings, and ensuring an adoption plan means ensuring that the woman's previous or future babies might have someone there with them in the further to help take care of them, or be family when there may be no one else.

Parents that choose to undergo the adoption process need our encouragement, and they need to continually be surrounded by love. It is a very difficult process to walk through from an emotional standpoint. Who

---

10. Coleman PK. Abortion and mental health: quantitative synthesis and analysis of research published 1995-2009. British Journal of Psychiatry. 2011;199(3):180-186. Doi:10.1192/bjp.bp.110.077230

knows, during the process, when they get closer to birthing the baby, if they have felt supported enough, they might just change their minds and decide to parent. Wouldn't that be wonderful? Our actions and words influence others more than we know.

Let's join together to take a loving approach and make sure that any family choosing an adoption plan feels no shame. Through love, we can save babies and families. After all:

> When the fulness of the time was come, God sent forth his Son, made of a woman, made under the law, to redeem them that were under the law, that we might receive the adoption of sons. (Galatians 4:4-5)

We, as Christians, have been adopted through Christ Jesus.

Adoption is biblical. When you think about it, Christians were all adopted. I don't think I have ever met a Christian who is against adoption, but sometimes people say things that shame people from adopting or shame mothers for wanting to give their baby another family through adoption. Someone once told me that I was the first and only person that had ever told her that she made a good decision—that she was actually being a good mother by choosing to give her baby the chance. We don't like to say "giving your baby up for adoption" because they are not giving their baby up. They are giving the child a chance at life.

I was praying and asking Holy Spirit what to say, and one of the things He said to me was that every kid was born with a *purpose* and with a *destiny*. Sometimes their parents do not have the ability to help them in the current state they are in and with the oppression the Enemy has on them through drugs, addiction, mental disorders, etc. That is oppression, and it can prevent someone from fulfilling their calling as a Christian or as a non-Christian. The devil's whole purpose is to steal from you, to kill you, and to destroy your life's calling. What God told me was that demons will stop the parents from fulfilling their calling, and in turn, that will make it harder for a child to be able to fulfill their calling.

When you adopt a child, you have just taken on a responsibility of helping another human being reach their calling in Christ. That is a great reward. That is a great treasure. Many people who have gone up to heaven and came back say that the kids that are up there are begging to come down here and be a human spirit. They want to come down and be Christians. They want to come down and worship God the way we do—where they get to choose.

The book of Psalms tells us that not only are children a gift from God but that children are a reward from Him. That word for reward actually is talking about *compensation* for a person who has done hard work or a hard day's labor. It's like getting your pay for doing a job well done. When you get a child, yes, it is going to cost you, but there is so much reward that comes from raising children. There are precious memories you will never have if you do not have kids. Ask anybody. It does not matter if they are adopted or if they are biological; you are gonna love that child no matter what because you are the parent, and you are going to have amazing memories. They will grow up, and they will call you Mom or Dad. Now that is an honor and privilege from God.

Some women who consider adoption as an option are people who are focused on their life goals, whether that means finishing school or continuing in the career path they are on. I know that one woman I talked to had just gotten a manager position at work, and she had three other kids at home whom she was fully providing for by herself. This was a good option for her because she did not know how she would feed another mouth, get the manager position at her job, and care for a newborn baby.

Adoption is a great option, not only for the birth mother, but also for the parents that get to adopt the baby. It is the ability to give a family fulfillment. There are many families who try and would give anything to have a child. I encourage you to get in Scripture and see what it says about adoption. The Bible is very clear about choosing life, and the Bible talks to us about adoption. If you are reading this and thinking that you may not be able to care for the baby inside of you, please reconsider. Adoption is a healthy option.

Where do we see adoption in the Bible?

We actually see adoption in the Bible in several different places. In fact, it is all throughout the Bible.

> I will be a father to you and you will be my sons and daughters, says the Lord Almighty.
> (2 Corinthians 6:18)

> Religion that God our Father accepts as pure and faultless is this: to look after orphans and widows in their distress and to keep oneself from being polluted by the world.
> (James 1:27)

> But when the set time had fully come, God sent his Son, born of a woman, born under the law, to redeem those under the law, that we might receive adoption to sonship.
> (Galatians 4:4-5)

We see all throughout the Bible that it is godly and biblical to adopt and take care of someone who is without a father and mother—someone who is an orphan. When you think about it, God told the Pharisees that they were of their father, the devil. Everyone says we are all God's children, but we are not all God's children. Jesus said that some of them were Satan's children. You have to be *adopted* into the family.

> Yet to all who did receive him, to those who believed in his name, he gave the right to become children of God. (John 1:12)

I was praying, as I said earlier, and the Holy Spirit showed me Psalm 68:5:

> A father to the fatherless, a defender of widows, is God in his holy dwelling.

What I really love about that is that we are the holy dwelling of God now, right? This was talking about being in heaven, and that is where God dwells, but now the Holy Spirit is here on earth, in us. We abide in Him as He abides in us. He lives in us.

Scripture says that we are the temple of God and that the Spirit of God dwells within us. Think about that. It says in Psalm 68:5, a Father to the fatherless, a defender of widows, is God in His holy dwelling. Then it says the Spirit of God dwells in *us*. This was before Jesus. Think about that. Before there was Jesus, He was up there; He was still being a Father. He was still adopting people that were not His children yet, but they were His Children in one sense: He was taking care of them. It is His nature to be a father. Therefore, it should be in our nature to be parents. It should be natural for us to want to be parents. Some people do not want to be parents, and Jesus says for those who do not want to get married to remain abstinent for the sake of serving God. It is a calling, and it is fine for them to choose that. But we were born and designed to bear fruit; and children are fruit.

If God, as a Father to the fatherless, is in His holy dwelling, then that means He is in you—you and I are His holy dwelling. So that also means that He wants to be a Father or a parental figure through us. He gives us the chance to display His nature through us. That is something that will not only transform our life, but it is going to transform how we view being a parent and how we view adoption. If you get ahold of that, it will completely transform your walk with Jesus.

Remember, some people are not considered sons of God. You do not become a son of God in this aspect until you become a Christian. When you are taking care of people, when you are praying for people, when you are casting out devils, when you are speaking in tongues, when you are giving prophetic words, when you are exhorting one another, when you are giving words of wisdom and words of knowledge, discerning between the spirits, helping people, and loving each other, you are displaying the nature, character, and power of God. You are displaying Fatherly attributes. Just by being a Christian, you can have tremendous influence. Even if you are not going through the legal process to adopt someone, you could be a father to them and not even know it.

Peter adopted Mark and called him "my son." I am pretty sure that means he adopted him because Mark was not his biological son. Paul referred to Onesimus as his son whom he bore well in chains. Onesimus in Greek means "one who has become useful." Paul said, "While he was useless to you before, now he has become useful to me" (Philemon 10-11). The name that he gave him was a spiritual name, saying he was useful—a son, essentially. Adoption is biblical, and we have been adopted into Christ.

We have been grafted into the family of God, which means we have been adopted. We are unnatural branches on the natural vine, essentially. For us to be grafted in means that someone had to remove a branch and then put in a new branch. What they do is cut into the bark of the tree itself and make a little opening. Then they put the new branch in there and wrap it up with cloth or tape. The branch will be accepted by the vine, and it will grow as a new branch on that tree. We call it a family tree. You can actually add people to your family. They grow into your family tree and become branches of your family. It doesn't matter if they were biological or non-biological.

Technically, Joseph adopted Jesus. Esther was adopted by her cousin Mordecai. Moses was adopted. We read several instances in the Bible where major key players who changed history, nations, and now the world were adopted.

We are adopted in Jesus to the point where He has washed our bloodline clean. That means that when your doctor asks, "Do you have a family history of diabetes?" or whatever it may be, I say, "No, I do not. I have none of it." They may say to me, "I know for a fact that your mother has this, this, and this," but I do not have her blood now. The blood that runs through my veins is the blood of Jesus.

This reminds me of former friends of mine who were down in New Orleans in the old part of town. They were going past one of the main streets, and someone came up to them and asked if he could drink their blood. My friend looked him in the eye and said, "This is the blood of Jesus." The guy just jumped up in the air, and according to him, transformed and flew away—he just disappeared.

Moses name is *Moshe* in Hebrew, which means to be *drawn out*. Your name is significant too. Think about this. It is important to be deliberate about what you are going to name your children. Moses's name was *drawn out*, and he was drawn out of the water. That is why they gave him that name. Then he was drawn out of Egypt into the wilderness. Moses got married, came back, and then he drew the Israeli people out from Egypt. He took them back into the same wilderness where he had been hiding for forty years. Then he went into the wilderness for another forty years.

Isaiah means *God is salvation* in Hebrew. Isaiah preached about the salvation of God, which is Yeshua. He preached that how God will deliver His people. Ezekiel means *God will strengthen.* In Ezekiel 3, God tells Ezekiel that He will strengthen him and make his head hard. Then you have Jesus, whose name means salvation. What you name each of your children will be a prophetic indicator of what they are called to do.

Brandi's name means "pure fiery." If there is anyone who is pure that you will ever meet, it is Brandi. I (Robyn) am not saying that she is perfect, but she does everything with excellence. She tries to live the most pure life. She is righteous, and she is holy. She has been doing that since she was a child. It actually helps me to be a better person and a better Christian because she is such a good example for me.

> The King will reply, 'Truly I tell you, whatever you did for one of the least of these brothers and sisters of mine, you did for me.' When we care for those that are considered the least of these by society or by their family, we're caring for Jesus. (Matthew 25:40)The Lord watches over the foreigner and sustains the fatherless and the widow, but he frustrates the ways of the wicked. God is there, sustaining the fatherless. They're very important to him. (Psalm 46:9)

> He predestined us for adoption to sonship through Jesus Christ, in accordance with his pleasure and will. If we were predestined for adoption, legally and spiritually, then the fatherless are as well. (Ephesians 1:5)

> Speak up for those who cannot speak for themselves for the rights of all who are destitute. (Proverbs 31:8)

> Learn to do right; seek justice. Defend the oppressed. Take up the cause of the fatherless; plead the case of the widow. I don't know how much more you could do that, then by adoption. (Isaiah 1:17)

> And whoever welcomes one such child in my name welcomes me. (Matthew 18:5)

If you know a woman who is considering the option of adoption, one of the things that is really important for her to know is that a little over a decade ago, the majority of adoptions were closed. They thought it was better for the baby to never have contact with the birth mother. That is simply not true anymore. Most adoption agencies offer open adoptions. What that means is that you as the birth mother get to determine how often you get to see your child until they turn eighteen. That is huge because studies have shown that it is much better for the adoptive parents to have some type of a working relationship with the mother of child who has been adopted. It is better for the child not to have the shock factor later on.

It takes a community to raise a baby. The more great influences a child can have in their life, the better. Some agencies will even consider allowing the birth parent(s) to play a part in choosing the family that adopts the baby. You get to see their biography, what they do for work, where they live, how long they have wanted a baby, why they want a baby, if the baby will have its own room—all of those things and more. One agency near to us gives free counseling for the mom and for the baby for the rest of your lives. That is a blessing because they know how important it is to take care of you and help you process everything that is happening.

When you choose adoption, your health care is covered throughout the course of your pregnancy. Adopting a baby can be expensive, and having a baby can be expensive too. The way that Satan set up our current financial system is to keep people in debt.

As I said, in sonship, you have the ability to help a person walk into their calling. Even though you think you are choosing the child you will adopt, God actually chooses the child for you. He allows you to adopt the child because you are doing it in service to Him. When you do, you receive a reward from God, and in that reward is an inheritance.

This has a lot to do with children; they are an inheritance, which means they belong to God first, and then He gives them to you. Children are a living inheritance. I think the more kids you adopt, the better. You can raise them pretty much any way you want, as long as you raise them to know the Lord. I hope you raise them to believe in the fruit of the Spirit and teach them to operate in it because they have such great callings and great gifts in their life.

There can be a lot of complex social issues that derive from single family homes. I am not saying this to put any more of a burden on a single mother who is doing the best that she can. If that describes you, God will certainly help you. What I am saying is that it impacts children, and we can save them from these horrendous statistics.

One thing that people have a tendency to ask when you suggest adoption over abortion, is, "Why? So they can go into the foster system into foster care?" It is ministry when Christians adopt a child. When I see children, I see God's blessings. As believers, it behooves us to help the weak and the feeble. It is more blessed to give than to receive.

If you are a parent, you are giving your time and your money; you are making food and being a servant. Being a parent actually has its own reward system set up in it. I know there are a lot of Christian families out there who would adopt in a heartbeat. I can think of three people that we know personally who would love to adopt a child right now. I feel like we should probably have more Christian networks. I would love to see churches set up adoption systems to help get Christian parents in there to adopt babies. It is hard for some people to be able to adopt, and the help would be much appreciated. It is also a great way to grow these churches while giving the adopted child a loving community in addition to their new family.

In the body of Christ, there is a very big abolition of abortion movement, and that is taking care of orphans. If the parent wants to abort them, then they would be abandoned and even more orphaned to a different degree. I do think the body of Christ is starting to rise up to help because people are beginning to realize that adoption plays an important role in the prevention of abortion. It also plays an important role in protecting the mental health of the mother, whether she realizes it or not.

One of the biggest struggles and roadblocks I find is that some women say, "If I am going to mess up my body and go through nine months of pregnancy, I am keeping the baby." That is a hard argument to come against and try to give them a different perspective. You can get your body back into shape. In fact, it is better to be able to look at your body and know that you chose for another human being to be able to have life than to look at your body and realize you are empty because you had an abortion. It will help you not suffer from the depression, attempted suicides, and mental disorders. It lowers the statistics a little bit, but the statistics are still high. The best thing to do is keep the child and raise it. That is what gives the most stability as far as mental health is concerned.

There are women who fully believe they do not want children. I do know that the desire comes, especially if you choose to carry the baby to term. You have those pregnancy hormones that change after you give birth. You grow attached and bond with the baby. I did actually talk with one woman that said she just didn't bond, and she didn't want to bond. For her, the correct option was adoption. You do not want to be bitter toward your child your whole life. That is a bad perspective to have because children are a blessing; they are not a hindrance or a burden. You definitely would not want your children to feel like you don't want them. You don't want them to feel like you resent them. If you are a parent who really feels like you would despise your child, no matter how much you tried to work through it, then adoption would be a great option for you and your baby. You still get to have a relationship with the child if you have an open adoption. You still get to go about your life however you want to go about it.

The Greek word for *adoption* is **huiothesia**. It means *adoption* or *adopted into the divine family*. It comes from the word **huios**, which means *son*, and then **tithemi,** which means *to place*—to be placed as a son. It means to take your place or your position as a son in the body of Christ.

Just because a child was not born to you doesn't mean that God did not intend for you to be that kid's parents. I am not saying that the parents who bore the child were not meant to raise him or her. That is their call. But sometimes someone else has to pick up the phone. Somebody has got to pick up the phone or pick up the call. You have the option to answer the call and help a child reach their full potential. You have the opportunity to help usher them into a position of sonship—to literally take up their role in society. This is literally life-changing, and it is world changing. Your bloodline is cleansed, and you can break the generational curses in their life by adopting them. When they become a Christian, the blood of Jesus will cleanse their bloodline as well.

You can actually miss out on some parts of your destiny by not doing them. God has written books about us that are in the libraries of heaven. They contain all of the things that Jesus has written about us and wants us to accomplish. You can miss what you were predestined for because you make your own choices. Look at the words "dis" and "disappointment." "Dis" stands for *distance*. You have *distance* between your *appointment*. When you are disappointed, you missed an appointment from God. You can miss your appointments, and you can miss your calling.

If a person goes to hell, does God not call them? Did God not want them? Did He predestine them to go there? No, but He knew what their actions would be. He gave them free will, even knowing what they were going to do with their entire life. He had written a book about them that said everything He wanted them to accomplish. He did not write that they would go to hell because, if He wrote that in their book, that is what would happen. He did not author bad things to happen to them, or for them to be sick or deformed. If He did that, then God would be the author of sin, and He is not.

Did you know that Steve Jobs was adopted? Did you know that Jamie Foxx was adopted? John Legend was adopted. Jack Nicholson was adopted. Faith Hill was adopted. Tim McGraw was adopted. Eric Clapton was adopted. Marilyn Monroe was adopted. God knows the family that each baby needed to be with. Many cases are sad stories, but most of them overcame adversity.

I (Brandi) have a friend who was adopted from Romania. She did have to go through some counseling to get healing from trauma she experienced while she was in Romania. Her parents adopted her and she just blossomed. She is an amazing worshiper who can sing and help lead worship. She teaches children, and she has a heart for adoption as well. I know many success stories, and they far outnumber the ones that don't go so well.

If you go through a reputable adoption agency, you get to be a part of that process, so you won't have to worry at night. You can develop a good relationship with the adoptive mom. A lot of times, the adoptive parents have very good relationships with the birth parents because they are grateful and thankful to them for giving them a chance to be able to have a baby and the family they longed for. You may even gain a friend through it.

If you go through the foster system here in the United States, you can pretty much adopt for free through DHS. Now, babies do tend to cost a little bit more, but if you go three years and up, you can basically adopt for free after you get a home inspection. That costs around $50, depending on where you live, and then you can go through the process.

There are people who will walk you through the process and prepare you for everything, even the hardships. They will be there for you for the rest of your life to help take care of these children. My heart is to not see any child without a family. If you have an opportunity, become a spiritual mother or father figure who can bring healing to people who did grow up in a family. They may feel like their parents abandoned them during difficult situations, or their parents were not attentive to them or abused them—whatever the situation may be. We can all step up and be spiritual parents to those God allows us to influence with our life.

Maybe you think you are not ready to be a parent. Honestly, no matter how much you think you are prepared, you are not ever prepared enough. If you are waiting for the perfect time, the perfect moment, all things set to be perfect, you will never accomplish anything. Very seldom is everything perfect. The only time all the conditions are perfect will be when we are in heaven, and I don't think there will be a need to be adopting in heaven. Kids up there have God and Jesus, but down here, we have the opportunity to influence and bless them.

I feel like the Holy Spirit is saying, "Yes, you can." I can hear Him saying it. Yes, you can. Your age does not matter. Whether you are in your fifties, sixties, or even seventies, you can adopt a child. Abraham was one hundred years old, and Sarah was ninety when they had their son, Isaac. If they could raise a kid at their age, then you can raise a kid at fifty or sixty.

I know that not everyone is called to adopt. I am not trying to make you feel guilty or shamed, but I want to say something to those of you who want to adopt: Yes, you can do it! I know that you are going to be a good mom or a good dad. The reason I know this is because you are a Christian; you are godly. We did not scare you away; you are still reading! The Holy Spirit kept you here for a reason, and if you have been asking for confirmation, now you are getting it.

You will make mistakes. You are not going to be perfect. But do you know what? You are not too old. You have not expired. You want to give a child a chance, and God will honor that. He loves you, and He loves the fact that you have a heart to want to bless a child.

> Whoever receives one little child like this in My name receives Me. (Matthew 18:5 NKJV)

What resources do you have or know about regarding adoption agencies in your area? If you attend a church, maybe you could consider volunteering to create an "adoption resource" board at your church, or if you are the pastor of a church, consider putting one up.

Chapter 13
How To Minister to Someone Who Has Had an Abortion

There are women and men who are ready to talk about it, and there are some who are not. There are Christian women and men who are ready to talk about it, and there are women and men that are not Christians who are ready to talk about it. We want to equip you to be able to minister to a woman or man who wants healing from an abortion. Sometimes women have an abortion without getting the consent of the father, and then the father has to deal with the consequences. It can hurt very deeply because that was his child.

Do not say to them that they murdered a baby. Do not say to them that abortion is murder, and if you had an abortion, you killed the baby. That is condemnation, and it is actually Satan speaking. If your heart is actually to bring healing to a broken person just like Jesus would, then those are not going to be your words. That woman or man is already hating themselves. When you bring up that it is murder, they already know that. I promise you that the Enemy has made it very clear to them that that is what they've done. Do you know what we need? The love of Jesus.

There is a right place, a right time, and a right way to educate people about that. They do need to be equipped to know exactly what happens during a procedure through a non-graphic video. Some people do need the graphics, but consider the person in front of you and the timing in which you are educating. I promise that if you are posting those things on Facebook or any other social media site, it is not preventing abortion. It actually makes people who are considering it run further away from Christians.

Let's say there is someone in your congregation who tells you that they have had an abortion, and they don't know how to get through it. What would be your immediate response? I would hope they are telling me this because they feel I am a safe person for them to open up. I would probably start out by asking them: What is it that you are thinking or feeling right now that I can help you with? What are your questions and concerns? What lies have you been hearing from the Enemy that make you feel what you are feeling now? I could assume, but I would rather let them tell me what they are going through. They may not be able to differentiate the lies of the Enemy from the truth.

I'm sure they will say they feel horrible and that they are struggling. They may say they feel like they killed their child or something like that. The one lie that we hear all the time is, "God won't forgive me because I've had an abortion."

Remember that a very high percentage of women who have had an abortion suffer from depression and some sort of mental disorder afterward. Be careful to not label anyone, and be prepared for the unprepared. It is important that we be ready in season and out of season so we will have an answer for those who are seeking help to get out of the bondage they are in. Study and ask the Lord to help you be prepared to minister to these women.

It is best not to assume that you know how they are feeling unless you yourself have had an abortion and healed from it to know how to help someone else walk through it. Don't assume that you know what they are feeling. They may just want someone to listen and to help them process their emotions once they are able to express them. Just being able to express emotion after an abortion is a very huge step.

The will likely struggle with severe depression after an abortion, but often, that can kicks in five to twelve years after the procedure. We cannot assume we know what they are feeling. Some of them may not even know how to feel yet. We want to ask questions to lead and guide them into opening up and telling us how they really feel, and then we can help them deal with their emotions. Just as we would walk through the grieving process with someone whose loved one passed away, we will help these women work through the grieving process as the body of Christ.

My friend Lindy said something that I want to give her credit for. She said that women and men who get abortions truly believe that they are backed into a corner. Even though they say, "My body; my choice," they really feel like they do not have a choice. They feel like they have to make this decision because it is the only logical decision they can see. It leads to them losing their soul, meaning their psyche or their identity, their mind, will, and emotions, and their mental health, and then they cannot move on and prosper in life. That is in the Bible:

> Beloved, I pray that you may prosper in all things and be in health, just as your soul prospers. (3 John 2)

It helps to ask reflective questions. *Are you struggling with this? What does it mean to struggle with this? Are they in a place of denial? Are they struggling to come to acceptance that it did happen?* This will look a little different for each woman. Are they in a severe suicidal state? Are they in a place of self-harm, or would they harm someone else? I see cutting in women who have had abortions because they want to inflict pain upon themselves. Satan tries to make them believe that because they inflicted pain on someone else, they deserve the same.

We believe that as soon as these babies' hearts stop here on earth, they are present with the Lord. We also believe that if men and women truly repent to the Lord and become Christians, they will have the opportunity to be with their baby.

Women who have PTSD may have nightmares, or they could be driving down the road and all of a sudden have a vision of what happened in the abortion room, or of the pill they took and what happened afterward. We cannot assume that everyone deals with death the same way. This is a different type of death, but it is still a death. They must go through a grieving process that includes bargaining, but we cannot know where they are at on that track. It is always in our best interest not to make assumptions about people or what they believe.

I (Robyn) have been in situations in which I have made an assumption like that because I did not feel the same way that someone else felt. I tend to get over things quickly, but this is not to be taken lightly.

Ezekiel was told that his wife was going to die and that he could not mourn for her when it happened. He had to mourn the day before. He mourned because God told him he had to be strong. (see Ezekiel 24:15-18)

Or how about David? When God told him his son was going to die, he mourned. He was distraught. He was praying for God to not take his son's life. Then they came and told him the baby died. He got up, took a bath, and washed his hair. That's how I respond to things. Other people don't respond like that, or maybe they're just hiding their emotions and not wanting to deal with them. I explain these verses to help those of you who may not think helping people with their emotions is your strongest gifting.

One of the things that we want to help these women with is having some closure. I (Brandi) have experienced many deaths of family members and loved ones—eight close family members, from the time I was thirteen to sixteen—grandparents, first cousins, aunts, uncles, etc.; it was overwhelming. I was talking to Jesus one day, and I told Him that I didn't get to tell my grandma everything I wanted to tell her. He said, "Well, I'm right here with her, so why don't you just tell Me, and I will tell her for you?" I love that because I still do that to this day. We lost our dog, and I've told God what I wanted to tell my dog. I believe that Jesus told my dog what I wanted to tell him. That's one of the things you can offer to help these women bring closure into their lives. Have her write out what she wants to tell her baby. Then tell Jesus, and let Him tell it to your baby. That is still your baby. God gave it to you, and now he or she is in the possession of Jesus. What sweeter thing than to know that your baby is with Jesus, protected?

The hardest part is breaking down the wall. The wall of not wanting to think about what happened gets built up high, and they just want to go about their lives. But once you start asking questions that help break down that wall, up goes a wall of self-preservation. It can come in like an overwhelming flood to them because they have pined it up for so long. This needs to be done at the right place and at the right time—not out at a restaurant in front of their friends. Maybe you could invite them over for coffee or something outside of the church. They will need to feel safe.

I've heard one specific thing from several of my patients. They all say that it felt like a dark cloud followed them for the first two weeks after the abortion. It was just a big, dark, black cloud, and then life starts again. If the abortion doesn't have complications, they can feel like life starts to go back to normal. All of a sudden, they're getting to go back as scheduled. They go back to work, school, taking care of their other kids, or whatever it was they believed they needed to have the abortion to go back to. But then, all of a sudden, it's not worth it to them anymore. Once they start going back to life as it regularly was, those things don't matter anymore. They mattered so much before the abortion, and that can cause a lot of regret. Normal isn't normal anymore. We need to acknoweldge that. We need to help them establish a "new normal."

We help women work through that too, and the process starts with forgiveness. They can usually swallow that God can forgive them—He will, He has, and He will again. What's hard for them is to receive that forgiveness. If you get to minister nothing else to them, focus on forgiveness. Then focus on forgiveness of self and finding positive things about themselves to declare and to remember. Again, they blame themselves. Understandably so, but our job is to help them out of it, not push them deeper into it. It is interesting that they feel like they have a cloud around them for two weeks because I've noticed that with women, when you get pregnant, your sense of discernment and discerning of spirits goes up.

We believe that everything in life has a meaning. Some believe that not everything has a spiritual meaning, and some things are random, but it says in Romans that all things were created to point to the glory of God.

> For from Him [all things originate] and through Him [all things live and exist] and to Him are all things [directed]. To Him be glory and honor forever! Amen. (Romans 11:36 AMP)

Women have a sense of discernment when they become pregnant, and it increases in different ways. What they do not realize is that they are actually picking up on what is going on in the supernatural. Women have a heightened sense of smell when they are pregnant—even in dreams and in the spirit realm. If you have read our blogs or listened to our podcasts on the reality of dreams, smell, sight, hearing, and touch, you can they all have one thing in common: discernment. When your sense of smell is heightened, you are discerning something.

If you have already undergone an abortion, we want you to know that we love you. You are worthy of love. You are worthy of time, and God will love on you if you open your heart to Him.

We believe that if you ask God to lead you to women, He will fully equip you to help them. We will be here as a resource for you as well. If you are a church or organization, group, or even an individual, I recommend getting to know and make connections with professionals in your area who specifically help women and men overcome post-abortive trauma. You can go to the nearest pregnancy center and they will direct you to who specializes in this.

Chapter 14
The Role of the Church in Politics from a Biblical Standpoint

Should Christians be involved in politics? To me, it is a very simple answer. *Yes, absolutely*! But not every Christian believes that. I think that pastors and church leaders are put in a difficult place where the government tells them that if they have a 501 (c)(3), they are not supposed to be involved in political issues. That is exactly why we are not a 501 (c)(3) organization, and we have been very transparent about that. We do not want the government to have any control in what we say or do. However, it is crucial to teach what the Bible says about such topics.

There are pros and cons, but the point is that a lot of church leaders choose to be passive about discussing political topics for a couple of reasons. For example, seeker-friendly churches do not talk about difficult topics because they are focused on numbers and don't want to offend anyone. In our ministry, all we talk about are difficult topics! This is necessary because we want to be authentic. My (Brandi) heart is to disciple and mentor. I want to walk through tough situations and seasons with you like I am walking through life with you. There is no way to walk through life with someone without talking about what is going on in the political realm because it impacts us all. The other reason is that many people, including pastors, are uneducated about what is going on in politics and do not know where to start. They don't want to sound uneducated, or they are not confident in their understanding of the topics themselves, so they never address the issues.

Christians today have a very difficult time having a civil conversation when someone disagrees with them. Most of the time, if someone disagrees, people—including Christians—immediately start name-calling, degrading, and basically slandering others. For some reason, Christians seem to think it is okay to say negative, derogatory, mean, rude, hurtful, and disgusting things about Democrats. Most Christians are Republican, but not all Christians are Republican. You had better know that not every Democrat is an evil person. Democrats are children of God too. More or less, it seems like people just want to be right. Everybody wants to be right, and everybody wants to be heard, but nobody wants to listen and come up with simple solutions. This is nothing but pride.

Another explanation for why pastors may or may not have church involvement in politics is because they have both Democrats and Republicans in their congregation and do not want to offend anyone. If we get rid of all denominations and all parties and just teach the Word, then if they are offended, they are not believing the Bible. As a pastor, that is not your fault; it is their fault for not doing their own research.

Lastly, not every pastor or church leader is called to a maximum amount of involvement in politics. Not every church leader is called to run for office. Not every church leader is called to do extreme things in politics. Some are just called to teach on the topics because they have a call to pastor that church. Everyone has a calling, but as fivefold ministers, we are required to teach the Word of God. We cannot exclude and connote topics just because they are difficult or because they are considered political. We are moving into a time when "woke" churches are being separated from biblically based ones, so it is of utmost importance to make it clear and to know where you stand.

Leaving something out that we are supposed to do is something I am definitely not okay with. We may teach on a political topic and then never be invited back to that church again, but that is okay as long as we are obedient to the Lord.

There are many scriptures that very clearly show us several things. The Bible says governments should encourage good and punish evil. It says leaders should serve God and the people, not be in positions of leadership for self gain. Governments are supposed to safeguard human rights. God Himself gave standards by which kings should rule, and we should live. There's BOTH a political responsibility AND an individual responsibility. Therefore, saying things like, "Well, I wouldn't have an abortion, but I'm not going to force my beliefs on other people," is dangerous because we will be held accountable for not being involved at all to protect the lives of the innocent because it may cause conflict. There's just so much wrong with this stance.

There are two things in the Bible that I want to point out as scriptural evidence for whether or not Christians should be involved in politics. One is that before there were kings, there was a political system in and of itself with God as King. He is also the Prince of Peace, the Lord of Lords, and the King of kings. Second, He calls us to be the *ecclesia,* or *equity.* In Latin, the word means a governing body or system. This is not just a church or local body; it is the church as a whole, as a governing system. We are ambassadors now. An ambassador is a political figure in a culture and society who goes out as a representative of a nation or kingdom and enforces the rules and laws of the king in the kingdom. We are supposed to be doing that.

We are also supposed to be judges. We see in Exodus, Judges, and in Joshua that they instated judges, first with Moses, and it continued until Saul became king. The people came to them and asked for help with difficult situations and so forth, and they made verdicts and rulings. Now we are in that same position. We are the judges; we are supposed to be making judgments and so forth in the land. We must be involved in politics because we are *called* to it. We don't necessarily have to be campaigning and running for office, but we at least have to vote.

God can say, "This is who the next president is going to be," but what if He had a different plan? What if God sent someone who became president, but that was not His first choice? What if you wanted a godly leader to rise up, but He knew that Christians were not going to rise up and vote for a godly leader? God could say that a certain person is going to win the election, but is that person *supposed* to win the election?

If you get a word from God, it is your duty and responsibility to pray and intercede about that word. Take it to the Lord in private; talk to Him about it, and say, "This is what I heard; what did it mean?" Prophetic words are *necessary* for the body of Christ because they give us an indication of the direction the nation is going. We have an obligation. False prophets will be exposed, but when a prophet of God says something, God will back it up. It will happen. If we hear a negative word, we are supposed to pray so there can be a heart change, and there could be delay. Many times in the Bible, we see that the people cried out and said, "We want justice! We need reform! We need a reformation! God help us! Have mercy on us! Lord, heal our land!" We have been hearing that a lot now.

I had a prophetic word from God while I was praying in tongues, and He said, "You can pray, 'God, heal our land,' but in order for Me to heal your land, I do not need *everyone* in the church or *everyone* in the country to cry out for reformation; I need the body of Christ to stand up so I can use them to bring change."

The Lord told me that people are going to try to get pornography legalized in every state. This is important for us to know as Christians because it is our job to study what the Bible says about it. It is literally cheating on your spouse, and it is also cheating on God, whether you are married or single. It should *not* be legalized. It should be completely illegal. There are some things that we see on TV that are not considered porn, but God would consider it porn.

Yes, Christians should be involved politically. However, not only do we need more courses like this one to teach what the Word says and about how to get involved politically, *we must know how to hear the voice of God.* That is our moral compass and the foundation we need in order to be involved in politics. We need to give the world a moral compass on which to base their ethical decisions.

We must be very active because our adversary roams around like a roaring lion seeking whom he may devour (1 Peter 5:8). I promise you that the moment we are silent, he becomes active. That is not to say to do it out of fear, but it is our responsibility to know what the Bible says about these topics and use the Word of God as our moral compass to do what we believe. The Bible is true; it is not only symbolic. If you believe that the Bible is just symbolic, please reach out to us at firesidegrace@yahoo.com. We would be happy to discuss with you why the Bible is true and not just symbolic. If we do not fully believe the Bible is true, then no, we do not need to be politically active as Christians. We need to figure out what we believe and then step into that arena.

When Paul met with the elders of the church at Ephesus and he was summarizing his ministry, he said:

> I testify to you this day that I am innocent of the blood of all of you. For I did not shrink from declaring to you the whole counsel of God. (Acts 20:26-27)

He did not shrink back from teaching on any topic simply because it was unpopular. We are supposed to be preaching and teaching on everything that is in the Bible. The mark of the beast, the resurrection, and healing are difficult topics that we are supposed to teach on because they are in the Bible. We should present them in such a way that will spark conversation. Yes, we need to use wisdom, but we are talking about these topics. A way to be politically active is to just start. I exhort you to dig into what the Bible says about topics you wonder about. Refine yourself, and reconcile to God's Word. Begin healthy conversations out there.

We need to get involved in politics. We need to vote. It is our duty because it is one way we partner with God. It is an opportunity to say yes to things that are righteous and no to things that are not. We are in this world, but we are not of it. When people pray, "God, please go heal them," God says, "I told you to do it. I put the power in your hands. I said that, through Jesus, when you lay hands on the sick, they will recover." If you are not going to do it, then maybe God will do a random healing, but He put the power in *you!* You can't blame God for not doing something that He told you to do. We need to step into who we are and TAKE the land back, not just pray for it to be done from the pews.

We need politicians who are Christian to bring an end to things like abortion in their states. We need Christians who are politicians to help end sex slavery or sex trafficking. You are going to find out in the near future that a lot of politicians are involved in trafficking children, conducting women, and even men, and selling them into human slavery. It's called "white slavery," and it's not because it is a white person. It's called that because it is not spoken about freely; it's glossed over. It is like calling something a white lie, but all the while, a lie is a lie.

You need to get involved because that is what you are told when you run for office. I will tell you this from experience; nobody wants a radical to run for office. Nobody wants a person who abolished abortion instead of being pro-life to run for office. Then you have the opposite spectrum. You have the people who are so focused on abolishing abortion that they come against laws that would help save even 100 babies a year. That is not saying that we are not for abolishing abortion—we absolutely are, but I think it's important to know that because God has trusted us to live in a democracy, He trusts us to steward what we are given. He has given us the right to vote, so it is our job to steward what He has given us—the United States of America, our democracy, our obligation, and our right to them.

Blessed are the peacekeepers

Jesus said this, but He doesn't just want to keep the peace; He is not afraid of conflict. How do I know that? Because He told a church, "I see what you are doing here," and then He tells them there would be persecution coming against them for ten days. It was not sent by Him, but it was allowed by Him. He told them to remain faithful and strong until death. To sum it up: there is going to be persecution for ten days and you will die." People gloss over that and think: God would never say something like that; Jesus would never tell the church they are going to be killed. Yes, He would, but the reason I am saying this is not saying that He is vengeful. I am saying that He is not afraid of conflict. He is very aware of all that is going on.

The Pharisees tried to trick Jesus into violating a Roman law by asking Him if they should stone a woman who was caught in adultery. He had every right, according to God's law, to kill her, but God wanted forgiveness. The reason this was a political trick was because they went to the governor to get the governor to act because it was against Roman law for the Jews to kill anybody, even according to their lot. Even though it was justified, Jesus was still under Roman law, so he could not kill her. Even though He had a right, He did not do it. He also knew that He had already taken her sin upon His back—even though He had not done it yet.

If you want to start getting politically involved, make the first place you run to *the Bible*! Spend hundreds of hours reading the Bible to see what God has to say on the topic. If you ask, "God, what is on Your heart about this topic?" I promise He will show you. That is where you want to start. I used to keep a binder with what I believe about each political issue, and I did that because I wanted to write down and record what the Lord said, keep the research I found, and record my conclusion at the end. If you do not know where to start, start there.

If you are a pastor and you don't want to get into trouble for teaching on a political topic, something you can do is refrain from instructing anyone to support a certain candidate. You can say *Party A* and *Party B* without mentioning a specific party. If people don't know you well enough to know which party you are talking about, then there needs to be more education for them personally. Encourage small groups and questions between your members in a nonjudgmental setting, and create a safe environment for them to talk to you.

Seek the Lord for yourself as to whether or not you are supposed to be more politically active than just teaching on the topics. Ask Him if you are supposed to support or be a part of a parachurch group whose organizations fight for the abolishment of the abortion movement or other societal issues. If you feel like you are supposed to be a part of that, then you know to do that on the side. We can talk about it without being judgmental or derogatory, or lacking wisdom. With wisdom, we can effectively teach in love. Then, like Paul in Acts 20, we will be able to say that we are innocent because we did not shrink back from declaring the whole counsel of God.

Romans 13 makes it clear that God is for the institute of governments because they promote good and punish evil. However, if Christians do not continue to hold positions of influence in government, then how are we supposed to trust them to do good and punish evil? In 1 Peter 2: 13-14 we are instructed to be subject to leaders who punish evil and do good. But what happens when the government doesn't obey God's commands?

Let's look at a few examples in the Bible. Daniel's friends were rescued by God from the furnace when they disobeyed Nebuchadnezzar and refused to bow down to other idols. This means God rescued them when they disobeyed government. And in Matthew 28 and chapters 4 and 5, Peter and John were told by religious leaders not to use Jesus name, however, they stated, "We must obey God rather than men." Here they made it clear they could not obey who was in leadership, even though God had appointed the structure of the government.

Lastly, let's look at the story of Saul's death and how he told the Amalachite to mercifully kill him so he wouldn't suffer a terrible death. Malachi obeyed Saul, and though Saul was king, he still got the punishment of death for it. He was ultimately disobeying God, and God still held him accountable for His commandment that says "do not murder." This means God's law stands above all those positions of power, including the King himself. So, it remains important to be politically active to ensure righteous people are caring for our society and for our children. We can't just blindly trust that they are doing good and punishing evil, because non-Christians see our morals, values, and beliefs as foolish. They see God's ways as foolish.

Let me tell you this, ignorance is not bliss. I would like to challenge this: who decides what is a political and what is not? Is it a matter of opinion? If it's addressed in the Bible, then it concerns me, and I should be concerned about it. It affects caring for those who we are commanded to care for, such as the widow, the orphans, and the poor. It involves me. It involves you. I encourage you to get politically active as soon as possible.

About the Authors

Robyn and Brandi Cunningham are the founders of Fireside Grace, which was birthed to help individuals, ministries, and cities live to their full potential through Christ-based discipleship. Using the gifts of the Spirit, they teach truth to bring clarity to the body of Christ on issues that seem confusing in this modern age. They have a YouTube channel called Fireside Grace Ministries.

The Cunningham's goal to is to guide the church body by connecting the ethics, values, character, and morals of our ancestors into the present and future generations by creatively bringing the wisdom of the past, the wisdom of the Ancient of Days, and the wisdom of our elders into the present—and bridging the gaps of the generations in between. Together, Robyn and Brandi cover topics such as current issues, dream interpretation, learning how to hear God's voice, anointing, slaying sacred cows, and much more.

Robyn and Brandi are ordained under Michael French with Patria Ministries. They have been involved with various areas of ministry for the last ten years and travel full-time, writing, speaking, and leading worship together. They minister very often to families considering abortion, helping them feel safe and supported enough to choose to parent, with a firm belief in the importance of teaching about the family unit. Brandi does professional life coaching and is a dog trainer, and believes that all dogs deserve a chance. The Cunninghams are based out of Arkansas, run an animal sanctuary, and have incredible children.

To contact the Cunninghams, visit www.FiresideGrace.com.

Subscribe to their YouTube channel: Tomorrow's Headlines, Today!
https://www.youtube.com/@tomorrowsheadlinestodayfir7975

Fireside Grace Int'l
FiresideGrace@yahoo.com

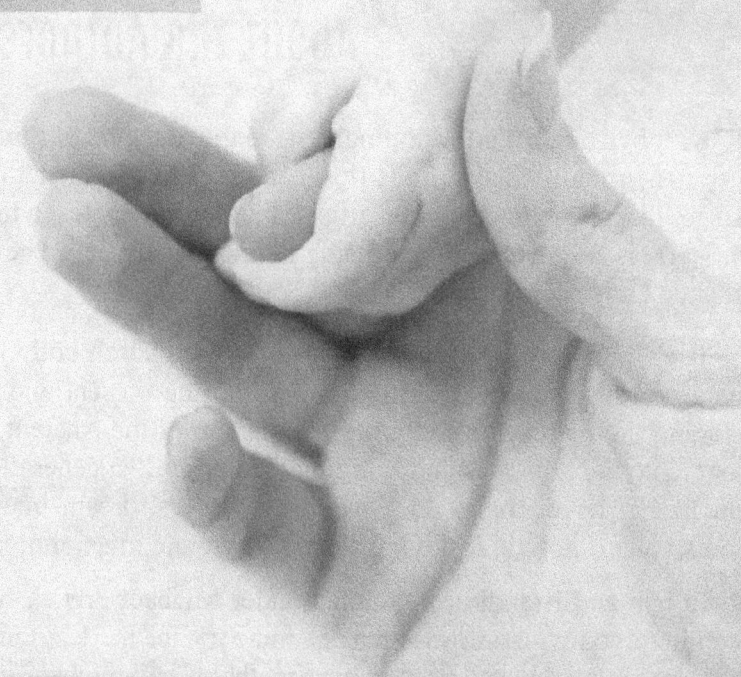

Ultimate Course on Abortion Prevention & Intervention

SPECIAL OFFER!

FREE Course taught to your organization and members to prepare the church regarding the topic of abortion.

80% of the women that have abortions claim to be Christian. THIS is what we're doing about it!

For more information, or to get a course scheduled please email us or visit www.FiresideGrace.com/abortion-prevention

Together, we can save the next generations. Apart, we can't.

Other Books by the Authors

The Pathway to Transcendent Peace

You can experience peace and joy DAILY. Right here, right now! This book contains the information that's going to set you and so many others FREE from EVERYTHING that holds you back from TOTAL immersion in the peace of the Lord!

For too long, Satan has kept us from being consistently in a place of peace that surpasses understanding. Join me as we begin to recognize and get free from peace robbing behaviors, and developing habits that will forever keep us in that perfect place of Shalom peace.

The Mark of the Beast

The Bible has proven to be the most historically accurate book ever written. Job talked of the water cycle and the earth floating over nothing in space; Isaiah revealed that the earth is round, Amos prophesied that men would be about to travel into space or into to the depths of the ocean. This timeless text has foretold scientific marvels and societal shifts millennia before their time. Within the pages of this book lie revelations that challenge the very fabric of our understanding—exposing the truth behind dinosaurs, demons, and even extraterrestrial encounters. Discover the origins of the mark of the beast, unravel the mysteries of humanity's primal past, and confront the chilling prophecies that herald our future. Are you ready to confront the secrets that have been concealed for centuries? Take the plunge into this extraordinary narrative and prepare to see the world in a new light in *The Mark of the Beast*.

www.ingramcontent.com/pod-product-compliance
Lightning Source LLC
Chambersburg PA
CBHW081501070526
44586CB00019B/2453